In a world of pretentiousness, false representation, and fake personas, it is truly refreshing to find a voice who is willing to be unapologetically authentic and honest. As I read Malfunctioning Man, I was compelled to re-evaluate my life as a person who says he is a man of God.

Jeffery challenged me to be better and build a better relationship with God. I was struck by the juxtapositions of the children of Israel and their need to create false gods in the object of golden calves and modern man's need to do the same. Today, we worship the false gods in the symbols of material possessions and brand names. He deals with real issues that are pervasive in our society today.

I applaud him for writing this book and creating a candid conversation about man and his relationship with GOD.

Ken Canion
Transformation Specialist

I believe men are in a desperate search of what it means or what it takes to be a fully functional man, but far too many men end their search as cheap copies and settle to simply be a malfunctional man which is embraced and celebrated by our culture. The Malfunctioning Man is a compelling read which provides both a road map to manhood as well as a transformational example in the person of Jesus Christ. Although a little verbose in some areas, the author has defended his stated positions with what he believes to be the final authority and the ultimate arbitrator of truth, The Bible.

As a practicing Christian and a seminary student I agree with many of his positions. Jeffery has passionately conveyed these truths with seminary depth, dinner table and relevant application. A short read, I recommend this book for any man who yearns to be all the man that God has created him to be. To paraphrase one of lines from my favorite chapter, Noise: "We have to also accept that the word of GOD is the truth. Only in this can we began to filter out the noise and decide to live by these truths and accept them as the standard of life".

Christopher Cooke
Founder of Called to Provide and
Editor in Chief of The Financial Call

The Malfunctioning Man is a must read for any man making a conscious effort to walk with God. It explains the correct thought patterns to spiritual success and the pit falls of the ego in such profound, provocative and experiential ways, that anyone looking for more understanding on how to walk in a right relationship with God will find The Malfunctioning Man a gift that keeps on giving through the spirit of God.

Michaelangelo Wolfe
Creative director Wolfe media - Producer Dirt sound

THE
MALFUNCTIONING
MAN

THE
MALFUNCTIONING
MAN

INSIGHTS FOR WALKING IN GOD'S TRUTH

Jeffery L. Cleveland

Art direction: Jeffery L. Cleveland
Cover design: Michael Angelo Wolfe
Editor: Natalie M. Cleveland

Book Layout & eBook Conversion by manuscript2ebook.com

First Printing January 2019 / Printed in the United States of America

You can only really share the story after you have taken the journey.
It is important to take the journey so that you can tell the story.
You shouldn't tell the story until you have taken the journey.
So take the journey, so you can tell the story with passion.

-JEFFERY CLEVELAND, 2019-

CONTENTS

Foreword

A dam and Eve were created as perfect beings, with a most wonderful home-environment in the Garden of Eden and with a future that was beyond their imagination. They were given the DNA Code to be able to produce every culture and color known to mankind. Our first parents had the great privilege of enjoying a face-to-face relationship with God, interacting peaceably with all other creatures and life-forms and, of course, enjoying each other while being fruitful and multiplying themselves through their offspring. Oh, what an existence they had! There was no "mal" in their functioning.

In Genesis chapter 3, trouble entered their Paradise; as Satan used the serpent to launch an attack against Adam and Eve. Satan accused God of withholding valuable information from them, deceiving them, playing with their minds and telling them outright lies. The Enemy brought such suspicion upon God and His integrity that Adam and Eve believed him. Not only did they believe the Enemy; they actually placed the same faith they had in God, in the Enemy. Doing so had a very profound effect upon them. Adam and Eve were so affected, their DNA was altered. Though their children were born as creatures in the image of God, their children and all persons thereafter, entered this life as "Malfunctioning Men and Women"; existing far, far, beneath God's best for them.

Jeffery L. Cleveland has done a marvelous job at articulating these issues. In this volume, he has expounded upon the wonder and majesty of mankind's creation and of his slump into sin, sickness and death. This author takes us into the peaks and valleys of the human experience. Not only has Jeffery given great clarity to the human condition, he goes into great depth in articulating the solution to our present state as occupants of this planet and our common conditions and mutual afflictions. Jeffery also does admirably in connecting Scripture to his contentions about God and about us earthlings.

You are blessed to have The Malfunctioning Man before your eyes and you will become far more blessed as you Read it with your Mind, Knead it with your Heart and Heed it with your Daily Walk!

Dr. Michael D. Woods
CEO of Ministry with Excellence, LLC
President of MWE School of Ministry, INC
www.mwenow.com

ACKNOWLEDGEMENTS

I thank GOD, the ALMIGHTY FATHER, for speaking to my heart about how to bring people together and making it clear to me that He has already made a way for us since the beginning. I am thankful to the many preachers, teachers, bishops, pastors and madmen who have poured into my life. For some reason there has always been someone willing to share their heart and story with me. Henrietta Turnquest, Frank Brown and Percy Butler did it early in my life and let me see behind the curtain on what makes excellence possible. I want to thank my brothers John and Deuntray for showing me love and camaraderie unparalleled by other folk and truly holding on to what it means to be brothers. I know I can always count on you guys to do what you believe the LORD has compelled you to do (whether it is what I want or not).

I need to thank Cynthia Smith. You took me out of Remedial Language Arts, moved me to AP Literature, and expanded my horizons. You had a poster in the English Lit. office that read 'Knowledge is given out here, bring your own container.' You enlarged mine. Thank you, Ms. Smith, for demonstrating excellence and demanding it. I am also appreciative to Escluveski, Travis and T Dott for convincing me that this book could be written, inspiring me by their own literary works. I want to thank Jessestephen, and Big Mike for posing questions that caused me to search deep for answers.

I appreciate Randy White, Chris Cook, and Ivan Maddox for being sounding boards that I could call up, read portions, and ask, "Does this make sense?" And, I am especially appreciative to Ivan who would say "well, no," when appropriate. I am thankful to Billy Milam who, when I discussed my heart about writing this book, challenged me to complete it. I would also thank Nat and Joshua who listened to me read paragraphs out loud to ensure I had parity and flow. I thank Miles who was motivation to me, as I always want to make him proud and show what hard work can do.

To my Mother who showed me that the standards I live by have to be above what is common to man. She worked her butt off to prove it, while maintaining a clean house, and constantly moving ahead in life. (She ain't no joke.) I need to thank Kenneth Canion and Valerie Burton for giving me guidance on what to do with the book after it was written. I want to thank Natalie Cleveland, again, for being encouraging and for all her help as I learned how to write and actually taking the time out to do it. Thanks to all. I dedicate this book to my Grandmother Lola Kate Davidson, the sweetest and toughest person I have ever known. She gave survival instructions when times were hard and love when it was needed.

PREFACE

I am no preacher or prophet. I have many areas in my life the LORD is working on, and I am learning to yield. I make a lot of mistakes, but I believe in the Word of GOD and the power it has. I have spent decades in churches, reading and talking with people and have decided to share some insights that I have experienced. There have been some great moments in my life that revealed the love of GOD and his grand creation for me to enjoy, and there have been some deeply fleshly moments that have left me feeling small and worthless. In the midst of this expansive range of being, I have learned that we have more in common than we care to admit (humans, that is). We all have the same Creator, who created this singular spinning ball in space for us to live, love, and learn upon.

I don't have a degree in anything, as of the writing of this book, but I have had a lot of experiences, so many experiences that one might suggest I have Munchausen syndrome, should I began to recant them all. I have had interactions and deep conversations with people in all walks of life, many varied ethnicities and socio economic backgrounds, and very few things beat a good story or a heartfelt conversation. It is saddening that these types of conversations are becoming scarce as we text and instant message each other more than I care for. I had someone ask me today to tell them how I felt about a topic using a GIF only for my response. We are shrinking down stations within us that are there for us to take in copious amounts of information and share them so they are awe-inspiring and perfectly relayed. We could use a myriad of methods to convey these thoughts and beliefs so that folk feel like they were present and understand them perfectly, instead of limiting to a text or a GIF. I wrote this book as an attempt to express myself and to share my heart in the hopes that you may understand what a great opportunity we have to love each other and live peacefully in GOD's creation, which is His perfect plan for us.

I am writing this book because I am compelled to do so, and I think it needs to be written. I enjoy the Word of GOD, and I am always moved as I see manifestations of the Word in the world and applications for it in my life. That may seem strange, as I believe the contents of the Bible are the Words of my Creator and the guide He has given us to enjoy his creation, which pleases him. Psalms 24 says *the earth is the LORD's and the fullness thereof, the world and they that dwell therein.* That pretty much sums up the Truth—that everything on earth is the LORD's, and He created everything. Psalms 149 says *for the Lord taketh pleasure in his people: He will beautify the meek with salvation.* I believe this speaks to the LORD's heart for his creation and his perfect plan for fellowship and restoration for those who choose to submit.

I deduce from these scriptures that GOD is not my enemy. He created me so I could enjoy the world, which belongs to him, and He derives pleasure from my joy. And, the only way that I can know joy is to know Him and to understand how to enjoy what He has created for me. We have to have a relationship with our Creator to understand the order He established for us, and accept it as Truth. Once the Creator shows us how to live with what He has created, we can partake of creation properly and with perfect fellowship. This is joyous—to live within the order of GOD, as He has created you and me for perfect fellowship with Him and His creation, that was created for us. Any other existence or endeavor to live life is based on vanity and pride, and will not manifest the perfect existence GOD intended for us.

Unfortunately, we are malfunctioning in this existence. With free will, GOD understood love was made perfect. In giving man free will man has to have choices and the LORD's grace and mercy provides through CHRIST JESUS's redemption for "bad" choices (that are contrary to GOD's order for creation) which are sins. Sin causes death. James 1:14-15 says: *"But each one is tempted when he is drawn away by his own desire and enticed. Then, when desire has conceived, it gives birth to sin, and sin, when it is full-grown, brings forth death."*

Chapter 1

MALFUNCTIONING

"GOD's ways are higher than man's ways," Isaiah 55:9. The LORD says, *"For as the heavens are higher than the earth, so are my ways higher than your ways, and my thoughts than your thoughts."* I can't even begin to expound on why GOD has done anything, except for what He has told me in His Word. Well, there is also what I have experienced in the order that unfolds in living life, verified by His Word. Whatever He says is Truth because He is the Creator of all things and has dominion over everything. I know that is a slippery slope as often times liars lead by saying 'GOD told them thus and so.' And, oftentimes folk, who do not believe they are lying (as there is no malice or evil intent in their communications), miss the deception because they do not have a relationship through the WORD (CHRIST) of GOD and with his HOLY SPIRIT to substantiate or validate their assertions.

Sometimes folk are agents of evil-sowing discourse and unbelief as they have rejected the Truth because they could not make it work to their own ambitions. They are redeemable through the shed blood of CHRIST as are all men and are not to be hated. You must have a relationship with the LORD and his Word to be led by the HOLY SPIRIT to shield their fiery darts and stand for Truth. Our goal should always be to show forth the love of GOD to both saved and lost folk. Ephesians 6:12 makes this clear, so we will not only separate the evil from the person but also love and fight to win back the lost through love. I am in no way suggesting a course of action toward them but a warning or acknowledging that GOD created all people. We must search ourselves through the Spirit, as we are fed by the Word of GOD, on how we are to interact with all men, which is love regardless of race, color, religion, sex, sexual orientation or place of origin.

Often times folks' beliefs are based on having strong feelings or emotions. Strong feelings do not make Truth. GOD speaks Truth through his Word, and the manifestations of his Truth are consistent with his Word. He is consistent in his Truth, as He changes not. The LORD says in Malachi 3:6, so *"he is always true and just, and we are in no position to judge him or his truths."* James 4:12 says, *"there is only one judge as there is only one that can create and destroy."* In the Book of Job (Job 38:4), it is asked, *"can a man judge GOD, where were you when he laid the foundation of creation?"*

GOD is sovereign, not because we declare Him to be, but because He just is. We create our own gods often, assign sayings and convenient truths to them, and worship them as they serve us. It has been the same throughout creation. Man has made gods, which he can carry, prop up, tear down, and place in high places, and then use them to usurp authority over others, as man reaps the benefits. Certain modern-day churches tell their members and visitors they are being obedient to GOD with the tithes, and GOD will bless those who tithe faithfully. GOD says in his Word—Proverbs 15 and 21—that He hates the sacrifice of the wicked, and He truly expounds on it in Isaiah, chapter 1:11-18.

> *"11 To what purpose is the multitude of your sacrifices unto me? saith the Lord: I am full of the burnt offerings of rams, and the fat of fed beasts; and I delight not in the blood of bullocks, or of lambs, or of he goats.*
>
> *12 When ye come to appear before me, who hath required this at your hand, to tread my courts?*
>
> *13 Bring no more vain oblations; incense is an abomination unto me; the new moons and Sabbaths, the calling of assemblies, I cannot away with; it is iniquity, even the solemn meeting.*
>
> *14 Your new moons and your appointed feasts my soul hateth: they are a trouble unto me; I am weary to bear them.*
>
> *15 And when ye spread forth your hands, I will hide mine eyes from you: yea, when ye make many prayers, I will not hear: your hands are full of blood.*
>
> *16 Wash you, make you clean; put away the evil of your doings from before mine eyes; cease to do evil;*
>
> *17 Learn to do well; seek judgment, relieve the oppressed, judge the fatherless, plead for the widow.*

> [18] *Come now, and let us reason together, saith the Lord:*
> *though your sins be as scarlet, they shall be as white*
> *as snow; though they be red like crimson, they shall be*
> *as wool."*

The LORD desires a relationship with each one of us based on obedience, not sacrifice. As the Word says in Samuel 15:22, *"And Samuel said, Hath the Lord as great delight in burnt offerings and sacrifices, as in obeying the voice of the Lord? Behold, to obey is better than sacrifice, and to hearken than the fat of rams."*

The LORD says throughout his Word that He blesses obedience. In the event that there is sin, then sacrifice can be made for the repentance, restoration can be made through the shed blood of sacrifice, and we can be made white as wool. When all men failed to walk in the manner which GOD had created, John 1:14 says, *"And the Word was made flesh, and dwelt among us, (and we beheld his glory, the glory as of the only begotten of the Father) full of grace and truth."* By this act, not only was scripture fulfilled and GOD's creation lived and died as He intended his creation to live as CHRIST is perfect, but the ultimate sacrifice was made so we could walk in relationship with GOD and not in sacrifice. Only through the blood of JESUS—the perfect sacrifice—can we be made white as snow (without blemish) or as wool.

The church, however, is still preaching sacrifice instead of having transformed hearts and establishing a relationship with GOD through CHRIST. I am writing this book to speak to establishing a relationship with CHRIST, learning how to effectively walk after the Spirit and not after the flesh, and learning how to disciple men to do the same. The Bible already does a perfect job of doing all this. I do not proclaim to have a better remedy. I am just sharing some life experiences and understandings in accordance to the Word to help shepherd GOD's flock along. I hope it is disruptive and causes a stir and manifests change in the Church and in the flocks' lives, as we are in a terrible state of affairs and the Truth is being convoluted intentionally to allow the manifestation of wicked, evil, perverse living that wishes to emerge from the shadows and be accepted as decent.

There is also the issue of the body (the Church) being torn as preachers seek to fatten their coffers instead of manifesting Christ-like folk who walk after the Spirit and operate in the joy of the LORD. The parishioners, or Christian folk, are always seeking approval and validation and are willing to pay for it weekly, since they continue to wallow in sin without belief of a better living. The preachers are like credit card companies constantly raising your credit limits instead of showing us how to temper our lusts and how to live debt free. There is no profit for them in the cure. Like pharmaceuticals firms, they believe in the cure, yet the profit is in the medicine. The medicine often times is a placebo at best (as are many pastors' sermons). This codependent relationship looks like the pimp/whore relationship or adds better understanding as to why a woman would sell her body and give the proceeds to someone who proclaims to care but bares suspect evidence. You work all week and give money to a church—no—a preacher who refuses to preach Truth and to develop you to being self-sufficient and spiritually sound. You're being pimped.

It is not my intention to write concerning tithing. I believe if you attend a church and you believe in their outreach and it is transparent—give. I believe we should give from the heart as compelled by the HOLY SPIRIT and not because of the bondage or yoke placed on followers by a lying preacher in the pulpit with his or her own agenda. II Corinthians 9:7 expounds on the LORD loving a cheerful giver who gives from the heart, not out of necessity or begrudgingly. This is an indictment that is often used to say that, if you are giving out of embarrassment or fear as opposed to compulsion from the HOLY SPIRIT (which is always joyous giving), you are not saved and can't really love the LORD. In truth you may not be hearing from the LORD and may be cajoled into fake obedience or charity, not having been compelled by GOD through the Spirit.

We must walk after the Spirit and not after the flesh. Galatians speaks specifically about being loosed from the burden of the law and loosed unto the Spirit of liberty, having the charge to seek spiritual pursuits in understanding the relationship of Saint, Savior, and our GOD ALMIGHTY, as we are encouraged in the scriptures:

> "13 For brethren, ye have been called unto liberty; only use not liberty for an occasion to the flesh, but by love serve one another.
> 14 For all the law is fulfilled in one word, even in this; Thou shalt love thy neighbor as thyself.

¹⁵ *But if ye bite and devour one another, take heed that ye be not consumed one of another.*

¹⁶ *This I say then, Walk in the Spirit, and ye shall not fulfill the lust of the flesh.*

¹⁷ *For the flesh lusteth (seeks to control or have dominion over) against the Spirit, and the Spirit against the flesh: and these are contrary the one to the other: so that ye cannot do the things that ye would.*

¹⁸ *But if ye be led of the Spirit, ye are not under the law.*

¹⁹ *Now the works of the flesh are manifest, which are these; Adultery, fornication, uncleanness, lasciviousness,*

²⁰ *Idolatry, witchcraft, hatred, variance, emulations, wrath, strife, seditions, heresies,*

²¹ *Envyings, murders, drunkenness, revellings, and such like: of the which I tell you before, as I have also told you in time past, that they which do such things shall not inherit the kingdom of God.*

²² *But the fruit of the Spirit is love, joy, peace, longsuffering, gentleness, goodness, faith,*

²³ *Meekness, temperance: against such there is no law.*

²⁴ *And they that are Christ's have crucified the flesh with the affections and lusts.*

²⁵ *If we live in the Spirit, let us also walk in the Spirit.*

²⁶ *Let us not be desirous of vain glory, provoking one another, envying one another"* (Galatians 5:13-25).

The LORD has given us direction and quantifiable results that ensure we are true to purpose. If we walk after the Spirit there are manifestations, and if we walk after the flesh there are manifestations. You can observe these manifestations and decide if your course and actions are on point.

It is easy to become a malfunctioning man. What that means is, it is easy to begin to operate in a manner that is contrary to the Creator's plan. The Creator blessed man with free will, and it is a special relationship when it is functioning properly. What does that look like? It looks like JESUS in relationship to GOD and creation, although his purpose was different in many ways. His relationship with GOD and GOD's creation was, and is, perfect. We are thrown off as we listen to preachers without fact checking against the Word. Even more so, because we do not have our own relationship with GOD from having established a prayer life and a Word regimen, we do not know what to search out in the Word. We are not disturbed by those things that are not GOD's Truth or don't line up with his plan for our lives because we have not studied and don't know his will for our living. We are subject to what the preacher says because we don't know any better.

We watch things on TV, listen to things on the radio, and accept things even in the church that are <u>not</u> Truth. Paul went to Thessalonica. The people went and got thugs to do harm to him (because they would not receive truth), but those followers were eventually moved by the Word. When he went to Berea, they searched the scriptures and saw the Truth of the matter. Paul goes on to Athens and stood on Mars Hill and reprimanded them for they worshipped an "unknown god." Paul expresses that the Truth is for all men as GOD has created all nations of men from <u>one blood</u>: "⁶*And hath made of one blood all nations of men for to dwell on all the face of the earth, and hath determined the times before appointed, and the bounds of their habitation*" *(Acts 17:26).* In these examples we see the three types of hearts or states of man in the church. In Thessalonica, folks were so steeped in tradition, that they lost the Truth and the relationship—their salt had no flavor. Then you have the Bereans who studied the Word, so that when the Truth came, they were ignited because they charged the doctrine against scripture and were awakened. As for the Athenians, they propped up their own gods and walk-in superstition, or rather man-made lifestyles, which spoke to natural occurrence, but denied the Spirit. So they dismissed Truth and Spirit, as they are worldly or fleshly.

The world is led astray because it has not been obedient to the calling of the Spirit of GOD that indwells us all to find the truth of our purpose and creation. We make ourselves and other things gods because we are compelled by the flesh to do those things that are contrary to the purpose of our creation. Not that the sensory input of the flesh is evil. It is being misused. It has become the "eyes" instead of the taste buds, establishing the vision instead of the flavor.

Our fleshly desires have become the ruling part of our existence instead of the means by which we accept spiritual truths. We watch food channels instead of harvesting our own sustenance and preparing it. We live to eat and to prepare for the experience as opposed to eating to live and having a moment of flavor that enriches. We are consumed with our lusts for the flavor without regard for the sustenance and the provider. The by-product is most of us have a yearning or desire that goes unquenched that we attempt to satiate it through food, drink, flavor, which can eventually manifests in sexual desire that goes unsatisfied or unfulfilled and becomes drug addiction and sexual perverseness. All those issues can eventually destroy the flesh with diabetes, heart failure, substance abuse, and sexual immorality, which cause us to kill ourselves or be killed by others.

That yearning is, in truth, your body malfunctioning and craving the instruction manual and the code to be set on the right path and to function in right relationship, which provides prospective. Many people suffer from cancer, apathy, and confusion as a direct result of what they have allowed into their bodies, hearts, and minds. Praise GOD ALMIGHTY that He is JEHOVAH RAPHA (the GOD that heals) and has made provision for healing every ailment through CHRIST JESUS. I know it becomes a threat to lifestyle as we think, 'Are we being asked not to watch TV, listen to music, or eat food?' Of course not, but we are charged to understand that if we do not understand a thing we are destined to misuse it. When Paul preached about eating meat that had been presented to idols, to some it sounds completely ungodly that a man would eat something that had been offered to a false god or in a manner that was not acceptable to the faith. Paul was in a different place and, because of his relationship and the truth in his heart that was incorruptible, the meat was merely meat. He offered it up to be cleansed, prayed over it, and gave thanks. He knew that the blood of CHRIST and the relationship He had would not allow harm to befall him. Even a greater dynamic of the relationship is that GOD knew Paul's heart and did not kill him dead for eating food that had been offered up to idols, as GOD knew it was only meat to Paul and that *He* was Paul's source. (That is a relationship.)

This is the important part about relationships in that they are two-way understandings and acceptance of the same Truth. If we do not know one another and have not spent time with one another, we have not fellowshipped to understand, and accept the Truth. Then in ignorance or arrested growth we are held to the law and to regulations that restrict us. The Word says in Galatians that where there are manifestations of the spiritual walk that person is rooted in the right relationship with GOD. There is no law governing those right relations and manifestations. Where the fleshly manifestations are persistent, then there has to be law to govern where your rights end and mine begin, *"least we bite and consume each other in our lust" (Galatians 5:15).* We get so caught up in potentially what we could be missing out on that we do not consider or grasp that the ways of the LORD are to liberate, not constrict.

All of creation was given to man and their orders on how to use and enjoy it are gained through experience and fellowship with GOD. JESUS walked in perfect fellowship with Creator and creation while here on earth, understanding the Creator was to be worshiped and not the creation. That's how He (JESUS) could speak to storms, seas, trees, birds, fish and men in perfect order as he was clearly free and understood his relationship to perfect order. CHRIST was not giving praise or credit to the universe, because it is the creation not the Creator. Most people can't control the family pet let alone speak to a plant -ref Mark 11:12.

So, how do we cease from malfunction? Is it possible to be restored to the creation that GOD intended for us to be in order to fully know the joy of creation? Can we live a life that is not full of doubt, fear, and uncertainty, constantly seeking to be validated by a world that is intent on using and pimping you out? Yes! As every Christian accepts CHRIST JESUS and allows him to come and live inside them, at that moment, they have received the new codes and manuals to be reprogrammed and to function in the proper manner. At that moment, you are a new creature in CHRIST with the strength, power, and possibility to live free of sin and walk upright before the LORD.

I used to think it was some type of evil joke when CHRIST would tell folk *"go and sin no more" (John 8:11)*. To the adulterous woman (a spiritual and physical rebellion against GOD, and also culturally irreverent), how does one just stop sinning when it has become so common, it is cultural? Romans 8:13: *"For if you live according to the flesh you will die, but if by the SPIRIT you put to death the deeds of the body you will live."*

We have been granted power over sin. Where do you get the will to do so? The will is in the understanding that it is best for you. It is in understanding that all of creation is meant to yield to the LORD, and does yield, when creation is not acted upon by man or evil manifestation of sin (which is killing creation). GOD's order is yet where spiritual manifestations— joy and peace—reside. When we yield to GOD's order that is made Truth in his Word (the Bible, not by most preachers like Jeroboam and the high places), we miss nothing GOD has for us and or our heart's desires. Our hearts are transformed to desire His will, which is best. No man can share this; it has to be revealed to us individually and confirmed by GOD.

The Jim Jones's, Branch Davidian's, Manson Family, members of Heavens Gates and others were led by dynamic ministers of lies, reinterpreting GOD's Word to hurting folk who refused to read the Bible for themselves and develop a relationship with GOD for themselves. I say this without reservation because, not only have I read the Word and their doctrine was not biblically sound, but they died as horrifically as they lied and lived, as sin manifests itself as a mockery of rebellion against GOD.

The problem is that you are in the wrong place, performing the wrong task, receiving input that has nothing to do with your purpose. You now have the power through the HOLY SPIRIT to break free and live right. You just need new sensory input and relocation data so you can operate in the power of the HOLY SPIRIT, which indwells you–where your free will and choices become essential. This is the moment where you have to decide that you will allow the GOD of creation to have His way with you. Lay down your life, surrender, and have faith. What this means is that as evil is made manifest to you and, as darkness is looming ahead of you, you will shine light in those areas and turn and run from evil. As you began to develop these repetitive actions here, the HOLY SPIRIT will begin to restore you to the proper place and change your perspective to line up with the heart of GOD who already indwells you. He will change your life forever.

Like any relationship, fellowship with GOD it is not just a one-time meeting that has a lasting impact, and then you cease from interacting with each other. It is important on a daily basis to reach out, have fellowship, and strengthen the relationship so that it becomes the most important relationship you have. With this you can use the sensory inputs of your five senses to experience the spiritual reality and to begin to enjoy life in proper perspective. Things are seen in a different light and take on new meaning as they are seen in proper perspective. The feel and touch of creation with heightened senses begins to speak to His purpose and creation. The taste and flavor of things are clearer in the sacrifice made to produce something for your sustenance and enjoyment becomes an experience of taste and flavor. While the sounds of creation seem to orchestrate above the synthetic noise and your awareness of other life forms, small and great, is a symphony to the ears. I remember seeing blues and greens richer than ever after deliverance service once as I was in tune and seeking the LORD in everything, and He was there for me.

The goal of this book is to share practices that make our relationship with GOD easier and to obtain a better understanding in line with Bible Truths to help us no longer live a malfunctioning life. The power gained through the HOLY SPIRIT will help you and others do the same. Rising up, dedicating the first fruits of your life to the LORD is not mandatory but it is fulfilling. There are a lot of best practices that help strengthen the relationship with our Creator. To wake up and praise the LORD for the gift of life and the opportunity to serve him sets the tone for the day. Then, there is the privilege to pave the way through prayer for others to impact their day and show forth the love of GOD. There is also time to be encouraged as the LORD speaks to you of His love for you and His plan for salvation, redemption, and eternity through His Word. These are rituals that have changed my life and caused me to see the LORD throughout my day as sovereign and real. No one can ever take that from us.

Chapter 2

The "God" You Tote

1 Timothy 2:5 states, *"For there is one God, and one mediator between God and men, the man Christ Jesus."* Man does one of three things when it comes to accepting GOD in his life. (1) He both accepts the GOD of the Bible and spends his life getting to know him and *His* plan for his life. (2) Man will create a god that does his bidding or is to his conception or liking, or (3) he denies the existence of GOD and exalts himself. Whether it is the universe or any other incarnation of imagination or choice, there is only one GOD ALMIGHTY and one Savior, JESUS CHRIST. There are not many paths to the FATHER only one. It is through JESUS CHRIST. John 14:6: *"Jesus saith unto him, I am the way, the truth, and the life: no man cometh unto the Father, but by me."*

When the children of Israel were in the desert and Moses had gone up Mount Sinai to receive the law (which was the provision by which man would have right relationship with GOD), the children of Israel rebelled and bid Aaron (GOD's choice for priest) to make a golden calf. They reasoned that Moses was dead or had just run off. In Exodus 32:1,

"And when the people saw that Moses delayed to come down out of the mount, the people gathered themselves together unto Aaron, and said unto him, Up, make us gods, which shall go before us; for as for this Moses, the man that brought us up out of the land of Egypt, we know not what is become of him."

(Exodus 32:1 KJV)

It took quite a bit to come to this conclusion, that GOD brought them out of Egypt after delivering 10 plagues, the Passover, parting of the Red Sea, manna from heaven, quails in the dessert, water from rocks and leading them with a pillar of cloud and a fire tornado only to leave them alone in the desert to starve and die.

In denying GOD and Moses, they immediately would have to resort to the manner of living that they understood to be common in the land they were dwelling in at that time. The relationship they had with GOD thus far was through the man of GOD, Moses. They had not established individual relationships with GOD to understand His righteousness. Moses had not written Deuteronomy or Leviticus; he had not even come down from the mountain with GOD's law written with GOD's own hand. What they were left with was their flesh and evil hearts seeking survival and satisfaction.

They surrendered to the knowledge they had of the customs of the area and of Egypt in rebellion. The children of Israel say to Aaron *"Up, make us gods, which shall go before us"* (Exodus 32:1 KJV). What they present in this statement is strong because what their hearts show is prevalent in lost folk even unto this day. It shows that we must often have a symbol of who we are outwardly that will influence the people who do not know us. Our golden calves today bare the symbols of Mercedes, Ferrari, and brands that have been established as emblems of affluence and prosperity. Possession of these standards invokes what economists call the Veblen effect, established by Dr. Thorstein Veblen. It means that identifiable brands warrant increases in prices establishing exclusivity that separates common people and the affluent (Lynne Pepall, 2016).

The philosophy goes on to explain how that belief influences the supply and demand curve, but we don't need that part for this point. What we do need to understand is that they speak before us and establish affluence. The "god standard" in the land for gods and worship was Baal the god of the Canaanites, often represented as a calf, a man with a calf or bull head, and occasionally as the sun (Pope, 2008). Back in Egypt, Apis was the bull god they worshiped. The Israelites chose the hellish symbol common in the area, and they kicked it up a notch by having theirs be made of gold. The children of Israel took their own gold in the form of jewelry they had commandeered from the Egyptians and made a god they could tote in front of them as a banner or standard. It was not a god meant to inspire moral behavior within them as the consequent reveling or partying after its creation would demonstrate. The first attempt man makes when he creates a god is to validate it:

"*4 And he received them at their hand, and fashioned it with a graving tool, after he had made it a molten calf: and they said, these be thy gods, O Israel, which brought thee up out of the land of Egypt.*

5 And when Aaron saw it, he built an altar before it; and Aaron made proclamation, and said, tomorrow is a feast to the Lord.

6 And they rose up early on the morrow, and offered burnt offerings, and brought peace offerings; and the people sat down to eat and to drink, and rose up to play." (Exodus 32:4-6)

They worshipped and made offerings, and then exalted themselves above it by doing their own will. Man does not want a god to serve but a god to serve him. Man wants a god he can have so others believe that it controls his will or establishes boundaries to his lusts. What I mean by that is, if a man can establish the attributes of the god he serves and have them justify his actions, he then is not acting of his own volition but is compelled. The god he totes has not only become a standard but a reason.

In any society we establish law that defines where one person's rights end and another's begin. The one thing that we set above the law is the will of God, or to be compelled by God. In the Bible we see civic law questioned by God's law often. Throughout the Bible men are compelled to do things that are not conventional as they strike out and build arks, leave their homelands, defy kings and rebel against customs in the name of the LORD. If you don't have a relationship with the LORD, you can't challenge the god they tote especially when you are being told that it is the same as the God you worship.

That's what Aaron did. Once he had made the golden calf, he proclaimed, *"These be thy gods, O Israel, which have brought thee up out of the land of Egypt" (Exodus 32:8).* So <u>you have</u> <u>not created a god</u>, but you are worshipping GOD ALMIGHTY in a new fashion. This is sin because man does not get to decide how he worships GOD. GOD decides and declares how He is to be worshipped. It is not that GOD changes, but different situations require different remedies. GOD did not send JESUS the day after Adam sinned (although He had prepared for the event, as CHRIST was with Him). He established law, relationships, covenants, dispensations, and administrations so that the penalty of sin would be known and the price paid to remedy it established as worthy.

When Jeroboam was king of Northern Israel, in his fear and insecurity, he established worship areas known as "high places" where he had golden calves set up and announced that "this is the same god that delivered the people from Egypt". His fear was that people would go to Jerusalem to the temple, worship, and stay. He believed that eventually they would decide they did not need two kings and have him killed.

> *"²⁶ And Jeroboam said in his heart, now shall the kingdom return to the house of David:*
> *²⁷ If this people go up to do sacrifice in the house of the Lord at Jerusalem, then shall the heart of this people turn again unto their lord, even unto Rehoboam*

king of Judah, and they shall kill me, and go again to Rehoboam king of Judah.

28 *Whereupon the king took counsel, and made two calves of gold, and said unto them, It is too much for you to go up to Jerusalem: behold thy gods, O Israel, which brought thee up out of the land of Egypt.*

29 *And he set the one in Bethel, and the other put he in Dan.*

30 *And this thing became a sin: for the people went to worship before the one, even unto Dan.*

31 *And he made an house of high places, and made priests of the lowest of the people, which were not of the sons of Levi.*

32 *And Jeroboam ordained a feast in the eighth month, on the fifteenth day of the month, like unto the feast that is in Judah, and he offered upon the altar. So did he in Bethel, sacrificing unto the calves that he had made: and he placed in Bethel the priests of the high places which he had made."*   (1 Kings 12:26 – 32)

Sound familiar? It is almost the same actions of the Israelites in the wilderness before the sacred mountain.

There is only one GOD Almighty. Everything and everybody else who proclaims to be so is a liar. As Jeroboam made a god to serve his purpose, he proclaims it to be the god of Moses. He knew the lie would not hold up by itself, so he had to get yes men, dress them up like the real priests, and have ceremonies and houses of worship. He had to make the show grand to persuade the people. Like the mega churches of our time, the truth is watered down, not preached in proper context, and established to separate you from your hard earned cash and feed your need for validation, while leaving you broken and unawares.

The use of grand bands and orchestration, choirs with video presentations, while lower- base folk are placed over ministries who barely know the Word but are disciples of the pastor. This is no different than Jeroboam's use of gods and idols to establish his own desires. So many of us fall right in line, too, with the belief that it is Jeroboam who will be judged for his sin, not the followers. I often hear people say, 'If the pastor is lying or is crooked, GOD will deal with him.' He will deal with you as well for allowing yourself to be led astray when He has given you the Truth in His Holy Bible.

The Bible is clear on this as it judges Israel. The Word states, *"...because of the sins of Jeroboam which he sinned, and which he made Israel sin, because of his provocation with which he provoked the LORD GOD of Israel to anger"* (1 Kings 15:30). The Bible goes on to declare to several kings that they had provoked GOD to anger because they had continued in the manner of Jeroboam the son of Nebat, who built the high places and established these fake holidays. It is also clear that the worship of these idols and participation in these holidays and rituals contrived by Jeroboam are counted as sin against Israel (2 Kings 9:9):

> "and I will make your house like the house of Jeroboam the son of Nebat, and like the house of Baasha the son of Ahijah, because of the

provocation with which you have provoked Me to anger, and because you have made Israel sin."

We have a responsibility to guard our hearts and our minds against false profits and practices that do not line up with the Word of GOD. I pray mercy and grace on people as they discover this, as it is not an easy task. Not easy because, to stand up against an established evil, takes heart. We are compelled to do so, as it is a spiritual thing to walk after the Spirit and obey it. To say it is not easy is to respond in the natural. As with the influences and social order, it is difficult if you do not know the calling of the Christian. 1 Peter Chapter 2:

"*1 Wherefore laying aside all malice, and all guile, and hypocrisies, and envies, and all evil speakings,*

2 As newborn babes, desire the sincere milk of the word, that ye may grow thereby:

3 If so be ye have tasted that the Lord is gracious.

4 To whom coming, as unto a living stone, disallowed indeed of men, but chosen of God, and precious,

5 Ye also, as lively stones, are built up a spiritual house, an holy priesthood, to offer up spiritual sacrifices, acceptable to God by Jesus Christ.

6 Wherefore also it is contained in the scripture, Behold, I lay in Sion a chief corner stone, elect, and precious: and he that believeth on him shall not be confounded.

7 Unto you therefore which believe he is precious: but unto them which be disobedient, the stone which the builders disallowed, the same is made the head of the corner,

8 *And a stone of stumbling, and a rock of offence, even to them which stumble at the word, being disobedient: whereunto also they were appointed.*

9 *But ye are a chosen generation, a royal priesthood, an holy nation, a peculiar people; that ye should shew forth the praises of him who hath called you out of darkness into his marvelous light;*

10 *Which in time past were not a people, but are now the people of God: which had not obtained mercy, but now have obtained mercy."*

The scripture refers to us as a chosen generation, a royal priesthood, a holy nation, a peculiar people. We are not supposed to look like the world. We must ready ourselves in preparation for the coming of the LORD as in Genesis 35:2 when Jacob bids the fledgling Nation of Israel:

"2 Put away the strange gods that are among you, and be clean, and change your garments.

3 *And let us arise and go to Bethel, and I will make an altar unto GOD, who answered me in my distress, and was with me in the way which I went.*

4 *And they gave unto Jacob all the strange gods which were in their hand, and all earrings which were in their ears, and Jacob hid them under the oak which was by Shechem."*

GOD appeared to Jacob after this, changed his name to Israel, and blessed him with legacy, which would include kings and land. When we have god's with us that we accept as gods, we cannot move forward in the favor and power of GOD ALMIGHTY.

Moses did not continue to cross the wilderness with the god Aaron created, and Jacob did not go forth with gods of the lands. What stands out to me is the Mercy of GOD in being GOD to a people who worshiped idol gods. The power of GOD's relationship with man becomes apparent as both Moses and Jacob bid their clan to remove the false gods and walk with GOD ALMIGHTY, and the rest of the land was filled with terror as they tread through amidst the power of the Almighty.

There should be a distinct difference between darkness and light, hot and cold, salt and bland, and Christians and lost folk. We have a responsibility to study the Word as the Bereans did and to walk in it. I used to have issue with the scripture that tells the story of the prophet sent by GOD in 1 Kings, chapter 12 and 13, where he was commanded of the LORD, *"For so was it charged me by the word of the Lord, saying, Eat no bread, nor drink water, nor turn again by the same way that thou camest."* So he did not eat when he was charged by the king who he perceived in the natural to be evil. Then there came a man professing to be a prophet (the Bible says he was a prophet as well), and he just flat out lied to the servant of the LORD and said:

> *"¹⁸ He said unto him, I am a prophet also as thou art;*
> *and an angel spake unto me by the word of the Lord,*
> *saying, Bring him back with thee into thine house,*

that he may eat bread and drink water. But he lied unto him.

19 *So he went back with him, and did eat bread in his house, and drank water.*

20 *And it came to pass, as they sat at the table, that the word of the Lord came unto the prophet that brought him back:*

21 *And he cried unto the man of God that came from Judah, saying, Thus saith the Lord, Forasmuch as thou hast disobeyed the mouth of the Lord, and hast not kept the commandment which the Lord thy God commanded thee,*

22 *But camest back, and hast eaten bread and drunk water in the place, of the which the Lord did say to thee, Eat no bread, and drink no water; thy carcass shall not come unto the sepulcher of thy fathers.*

23 *And it came to pass, after he had eaten bread, and after he had drunk, that he saddled for him the ass, to wit, for the prophet whom he had brought back.*

24 *And when he was gone, a lion met him by the way, and slew him: and his carcass was cast in the way, and the ass stood by it, the lion also stood by the carcass.*

25 *And, behold, men passed by, and saw the carcass cast in the way, and the lion standing by the carcass: and they came and told it in the city where the old prophet dwelt.*

²⁶ *And when the prophet that brought him back from the way heard thereof, he said, It is the man of God, who was disobedient unto the word of the Lord: therefore the Lord hath delivered him unto the lion, which hath torn him, and slain him, according to the word of the Lord, which he spake unto him.*

²⁷ *And he spake to his sons, saying, Saddle me the ass. And they saddled him.*

²⁸ *And he went and found his carcass cast in the way, and the ass and the lion standing by the carcass: the lion had not eaten the carcass, nor torn the ass.*

²⁹ *And the prophet took up the carcass of the man of God, and laid it upon the ass, and brought it back: and the old prophet came to the city, to mourn and to bury him.*

³⁰ *And he laid his carcass in his own grave; and they mourned over him, saying, Alas, my brother!*

³¹ *And it came to pass, after he had buried him, that he spake to his sons, saying, When I am dead, then bury me in the sepulcher wherein the man of God is buried; lay my bones beside his bones."*

(1 Kings 13: 18 – 31, KJV)

After I read this I was confused. I was like "LORD he delivered your Word as you had required of him. Then some old lying jealous prophet lied and had the man violate Your Word and suffer death. I mean, he called him out at the dinner table like, 'Aha! You defied the LORD now you're going to die.'"The man said *"an angel spake unto me by the word of the Lord, saying, bring him back with thee into thine house, that he may eat bread and drink water."* And he did it and died.

I have to remember two things to process this scripture. The first is I can't judge GOD, no man can judge GOD. His actions are justice, and his Word is Truth. Second, GOD gave that man a direct command and, until GOD told him otherwise, he should have stayed his course. That is, that the thing that is contrary to the Word that GOD has given you, it is to be ignored until GOD releases you from it. If GOD says in his Word that we are to worship him according to the book of Deuteronomy with Levites and temples and protocols, then that is what He means, until He declares something different. Again, obedience is better than sacrifice.

Once JESUS died on the cross as High Priest and the Cross the Altar, there was no more need for sacrifice, as he was both Priest and Sacrifice of perfect order. GOD shares his Word through Paul and Peter and other disciples explaining what the miracle of CHRIST means. He is the Word, so CHRIST fulfilled scripture, not contradicted it. As CHRIST fulfilled the law–the the whole law–and is the Word, we are extended grace as GOD sees us through the Son. If we create our own god and religions, we deny the power of the Truth that has been given us and deny salvation through CHRIST. It was also great to see later on in the Bible King Josiah, after finding the grave of the prophet (the man of GOD that prophesied of his coming 300 years earlier), left the grave to rest peacefully, as he implemented reforms, and dug up graves of evil men. (This was the prophet who was lied to and killed by the lion.) This act kind of served as redemption for me that, even though he was killed for disobedience, his obedience was rewarded, too.

I could go on. Take Uzzah, the man who tried to catch the ark as it was falling off the cart. He died because GOD said no one should touch it (2 Samuel 6:7). Then there is Achan (Joshua 7) who, when he was caught, admitted he had sinned. Though many were slain due to his disobedience, he admitted his sin and GOD was true to his Word and told Joshua so.

We have to separate ourselves, sanctify our lives and choose to serve the GOD of creation as He would have us serve Him, not as it is comfortable for us. Though we are not saved by works but through grace in the merciful gesture of CHRIST, the law is GOD's standard and JESUS had to fulfill it to be righteous. Only GOD can save man. The Bible speaks about these gods you tote in Isaiah:

> "*1 Bel boweth down, Nebo stoopeth, their idols were upon the beasts, and upon the cattle: your carriages were heavy loaden; they are a burden to the weary beast.*
>
> *2 They stoop, they bow down together; they could not deliver the burden, but themselves are gone into captivity.*
>
> *3 Hearken unto me, O house of Jacob, and all the remnant of the house of Israel, which are borne by me from the belly, which are carried from the womb:*

⁴ *And even to your old age I am he; and even to hoar hairs will I carry you: I have made, and I will bear; even I will carry, and will deliver you.*

⁵ *To whom will ye liken me, and make me equal, and compare me, that we may be like?*

⁶ *They lavish gold out of the bag, and weigh silver in the balance, and hire a goldsmith; and he maketh it a god: they fall down, yea, they worship.*

⁷ *They bear him upon the shoulder, they carry him, and set him in his place, and he standeth; from his place shall he not remove: yea, one shall cry unto him, yet can he not answer, nor save him out of his trouble.*

⁸ *Remember this, and shew yourselves men: bring it again to mind, O ye transgressors.*

⁹ *Remember the former things of old: for I am God, and there is none else; I am God, and there is none like me,*

¹⁰ *Declaring the end from the beginning, and from ancient times the things that are not yet done, saying, My counsel shall stand, and I will do all my pleasure:*

¹¹ *Calling a ravenous bird from the east, the man that executeth my counsel from a far country: yea, I have spoken it, I will also bring it to pass; I have purposed it, I will also do it.*

¹² *Hearken unto me, ye stouthearted, that are far from righteousness:*

> ¹³ *I bring near my righteousness; it shall not be far off,*
> *and my salvation shall not tarry: and I will place*
> *salvation in Zion for Israel my glory."* (Isaiah 46)

My GOD carries me I don't carry Him. Praise you LORD for your grace and mercy! I love the scripture where the prophet Elijah taunts the Babylonian priest concerning their pagan, idol god and says, *"Cry aloud: for he is a god; either he is talking, or he is pursuing, or he is in a journey, or peradventure he sleepth, and must be awaked" (1King 18-27).* Elijah had no fear of other gods of the Babylonian god because he knew it was a contrivance of the minds of lost folk. Elijah also knew his GOD was real through a profound relationship. He sought GOD and had a great relationship with Him. So many miracles are made manifest by GOD at the prayers of Elijah. Droughts were called, fire from heaven, healings and sustenance in the midst of dearth as Elijah knew his GOD was GOD of everything and he could call on Him and be heard.

Elijah was not an angel of the LORD or some other creation. He was a man of faith. His story is one story of what faith in action looks like. GOD has not diminished power since Elijah He is still all powerful. Why don't we see these types of manifestations? It is not needed. All we need do is believe in JESUS, and it is all fulfilled. We don't need to make sacrifice of animals or burn incense. We need to accept CHRIST as our Savior, and our prayers will be heard. There is more to that, as GOD says in his Word that, in order to be heard of Him, we must obey his commandments and love CHRIST:

"*11*And this is the record, that God hath given to us eternal life, and this life is in his Son.

12 He that hath the Son hath life; and he that hath not the Son of God hath not life.

13 These things have I written unto you that believe on the name of the Son of God; that ye may know that ye have eternal life, and that ye may believe on the name of the Son of God.

14 And this is the confidence that we have in him, that, if we ask anything according to his will, he heareth us:

15 And if we know that he hear us, whatsoever we ask, we know that we have the petitions that we desired of him." (1ˢᵗ John 5: 11-15)

Our GOD has proven He is mighty. He has shown mercy and grace and has made a way for us to have perfect fellowship and right relationship. We have to forsake self, die to self, and find life in Him. He is the GOD of all things and not given to our authority but is all powerful. We have to be willing to lay aside everything that will keep us from the LORD. Our understanding of comfort, ease, and success has very little to do with GOD's plan for our lives. We have to be willing to tear down the idols and strongholds and walk upright before the LORD. Knowing our GOD is Almighty and has power and authority over all things.

Chapter 3

THE GOD OF ALL THINGS

I recall when I said the sinner's prayers and was trying to live my life pious and righteous based on my understanding of right and wrong, I found myself looking to dissolve relationships where I had been engaging in sin willfully. I started cutting people off left and right and focusing on the likelihood of me committing sin at the influence of those individuals. I was a senior in high school and had been extremely sexual in my life, as a matter of fact, I was keeping score and in competition with several other guys. In high school the sexual partners I had ranged far beyond the normal numbers, and I was being praised by many for my sexual prowess. It had become my culture and sole purpose for living. Everything I bought to wear and the way I moved was part of my desire to gain sexual partners. To get saved and understand that said behavior was no longer permissible was crushing. I had no identity that I was proud of beyond that aspect of my life. Who was I to be subject to, and how would that bode with the crowd I identified with. I was resenting being saved because it seemed everyone else was moving in the opposite direction. Should I have waited until I was older to do this? Being saved did not seem proper for a boy of 17. I had to learn a new identity in CHRIST and establish relationships, after I found worth in myself through CHRIST JESUS.

This is the story of very many people. We create realities for living that are centered around fitting in or feeling exceptional. These actions and feelings are rooted in lies and contrivances that are further confirmations of our malfunctioning. In truth, GOD created everything on this earth for our enjoyment. GOD created us for His enjoyment. If you search the Bible for the word "enjoy" in most cases it is the result of obedience to GOD. People will enjoy the land, the fruits of their labors, and their children as a result of being obedient to GOD. The nature of obedience is order—to submit to the order GOD has established for your enjoyment. This works because GOD is the GOD of all good things. This means that in creation GOD established order, and as we choose to submit ourselves to this order. There is joy. The fruit of the Spirit is made manifest in our lives when we have power over our flesh and can force it to submit to the will of GOD.

I have worked with addicts or people who are self-proclaimed addicted to drugs, and when you ask them how they stop using drugs, I have heard the response 'well first you have to stop using drugs.' The proclamation means you have to get your actions in line with your goals (you have to get your mind right), and then you can figure out your cravings and habits. Cravings and callings to temptation are carnal (of the flesh). They must be addressed through denial and, when led by the Spirit, an all-out fasting and denying the flesh sustenance for a substantial period of time.

Flesh screams of its desires to be satisfied (which is a lie, flesh can't be satisfied), instead of tempered and used as sensory matter and not purpose. It is why, when we seek the carnal, we have to keep adding to it, as it never is fulfilling. It's not just sex anymore. It's strange positions, locations, role playing, masochism, groups, toys, same genders, different species, ages, and the variants go on and on because there is no satisfying flesh.

Let me reel this in though. I am not saying that there is anything wrong with sex for married folk. What I am saying is, if the sex is used for satisfaction of the marital relationship, there will be problems. Marriage is not merely a license to have sex. It is a covenant relationship that has an order for it to work well. The bedroom is not defiled. You married folk get down as you like; enjoy each other. Some folk just choose to live out of order, go through hell, and never adjust or leave each other. But, when done right and in order, marriage can be joyous. Flesh can't be GOD. GOD is not flesh and has no gender. He was flesh in CHRIST and is Spirit indwelling us all and the Creator of all things. GOD can't be tempted by the flesh, and He does not tempt folk in the flesh. Sin nature and the enemy are the desires and callings that lead folk astray.

Some folk will ask, "Did GOD create the enemy, evil, and sin?" They are perversions of what was created, and represent the manifestation of rebellion to GOD's order (which GOD allowed). GOD gave us free will, and when He created us with the capacity to deny and reject His Truth and live in anguish and torment absent from His order for creation, it is an act of love to have that choice, otherwise we are automatons—no better than puppets or tools. Noah could have jumped off the ship. CHRIST could have chosen to disobey the will of the FATHER. Because He didn't disobey, He is exalted above all; GOD's order for creation is sovereign.

We can't create reality. We can choose to live in delusion and call it real, but the order of GOD will manifest its causes. Here is what I am attempting to convey: the fruit of the Spirit is *love, joy, peace, longsuffering, gentleness, goodness, faith, meekness temperance (causes or results of walking after the Spirit).* The Word of GOD goes on to expound that, for those walking after the Spirit, there is no law. That is to say they are in full compliance with the will of the LORD already. Since they have chosen to live in compliance to the will of GOD, there is a promise made manifest. This is the order GOD established, and it is irrefutable, as it is truth:

> "*1 Whosoever believeth that Jesus is the Christ is born of God: and every one that loveth him that begat loveth him also that is begotten of him.*
>
> *2 By this we know that we love the children of God, when we love God, and keep his commandments.*
>
> *3 For this is the love of God, that we keep his commandments: and his commandments are not grievous.*
>
> *4 For whatsoever is born of God overcometh the world: and this is the victory that overcometh the world, even our faith.*

⁵ *Who is he that overcometh the world, but he that believeth that Jesus is the Son of God?"*

(1 John 5:1-5)

Because GOD is the GOD of all things and this reality we live is not happenstance. Everything has a place in the order of GOD. Things that are not protected are subject to the effects of other things. Leave your barbeque grill uncovered, it will rust, unless it is protected with rust-resistant paint. If the rust-resistant painted grill is left to elements, eventually even the rust-resistant paint will yield to the relentless presence of nature (faster in certain climates than in others).

I like this illustration as in GOD's order there is protection. Without his protection there is exposure and penalties each predicated on choices. Pay your bills on time and your credit score goes up, and you have greater access to credit. Paying on time shows your ability to manage life, which reflects good stewardship and greater opportunities generating greater benefit. There is order. It works in the opposite for disobedience and slack. That is to say that, if you do not pay your obligations on time, there are late fees and penalties. Your credit score goes down and you are considered not credit worthy, opportunities diminish, and your character is questioned. I often share this concept with my friends, so they can check for rust, mold, mildew, late fees, penalties, odoriferous emanations or negative attitudes as a barometer to how well they are handling their affairs.

There is something at the bottom of each negative outcome something neglected, reflective of not being covered, cared for, or managed well. It is intentional, as notification that change is needed. These issues or results are intentionally unpleasant. How else would you know something was rotting or unhealthy to consume if it didn't stink? The *stink* leads you to the problem so you can remedy the issue. GOD has established indicators. Joel 2:13 - 25 speaks of how the LORD and creation respond to his anger and joy for Israel:

> "*13 And rend your heart, and not your garments, and turn unto the Lord your God: for he is gracious and merciful, slow to anger, and of great kindness, and repenteth him of the evil.*
>
> *14 Who knoweth if he will return and repent, and leave a blessing behind him; even a meat offering and a drink offering unto the Lord your God?*
>
> *15 Blow the trumpet in Zion, sanctify a fast, call a solemn assembly:*
>
> *16 Gather the people, sanctify the congregation, assemble the elders, gather the children, and those that suck the breasts: let the bridegroom go forth of his chamber, and the bride out of her closet.*
>
> *17 Let the priests, the ministers of the Lord, weep between the porch and the altar, and let them say, Spare thy people, O Lord, and give not thine heritage to reproach, that the heathen should rule over them: wherefore should they say among the people, Where is their God?*

¹⁸ *Then will the Lord be jealous for his land, and pity his people.*

¹⁹ *Yea, the Lord will answer and say unto his people, Behold, I will send you corn, and wine, and oil, and ye shall be satisfied therewith: and I will no more make you a reproach among the heathen:*

²⁰ *But I will remove far off from you the northern army, and will drive him into a land barren and desolate, with his face toward the east sea, and his hinder part toward the utmost sea, and his stink shall come up, and his ill savour shall come up, because he hath done great things.*

²¹ *Fear not, O land; be glad and rejoice: for the Lord will do great things.*

²² *Be not afraid, ye beasts of the field: for the pastures of the wilderness do spring, for the tree beareth her fruit, the fig tree and the vine do yield their strength.*

²³ *Be glad then, ye children of Zion, and rejoice in the Lord your God: for he hath given you the former rain moderately, and he will cause to come down for you the rain, the former rain, and the latter rain in the first month.*

²⁴ *And the floors shall be full of wheat, and the vats shall overflow with wine and oil.*

²⁵ *And I will restore to you the years that the locust hath eaten, the cankerworm, and the caterpiller, and the palmerworm, my great army which I sent among you."*

This is a clear example of how, when Israel is in compliance, there is abundance. When there is disobedience, there is dearth and attacks. All creation reacts and responds to the order established by GOD. There is healing and redemption for the years of obedience and redemption from the canker worm—the caterpillar redemption from the ills of disobedience.

We have redemption of sin through the blood of JESUS and the opportunity to repent. This is the beautiful thing about the love of GOD and the manner in which all creation responds to His divine order. We can live uncomfortable, realize it is wrong and miserable, and eventually remember (hopefully) that a way has been made for repentance—turnabouts turnabouts, new mercies—so we can live upright in the world without having to continue to live in misery. If GOD was not sovereign, there would be no way out. We would be stuck in the mire, and tagged with the reproach committed eternally. People's hearts change, folk see things differently, and sometimes they forgive each other. All this is possible because GOD created all things and the way they operate or process actions. In Genesis, man was in harmony with GOD's creation and there was order established:

> "*19 And out of the ground the Lord God formed every beast of the field, and every fowl of the air; and brought them unto Adam to see what he would call them: and whatsoever Adam called every living creature, that was the name thereof.*"
>
> (Genesis 2:19, KJV)

Adam wasn't being bit by mosquitoes, chased by lions, or taunted by monkeys. There was nothing out of order. This is how the GOD of creation established order and set the framework for interaction between everything He created.

Adam had a job, a wife, and perfect fellowship with GOD. Rebellion, the essence of sin, brought about chaos through a lie, which was intended to bring about the death of GOD's creation. GOD ALMIGHTY shed blood, covered Adam and Eve, and set in place rules and protocols for living. This established a long purification process and set in place a series of interactions to redeem man of his failed order of obedience. This process afforded man the opportunity to live life in joy and experience life on earth and eternally in heaven through CHRIST JESUS.

Man has no predators stalking him in the food chain; there is nothing on earth that He can't be covered from or have command over. As stated in Genesis 1:26, GOD has granted man dominion:

> "And God said, Let us make man in our image, after our likeness: and let them have dominion over the fish of the sea, and over the fowl of the air, and over the cattle, and over all the earth, and over every creeping thing that creepeth upon the earth."

CHRIST, the perfect man, had dominion over all things that GOD created. This was the order man was intended to have but lost vision of this through sin. It is no longer a curse, as CHRIST through his crucifixion became a curse to break the curse upon men (Galatians 3:13). What does this mean? Romans 6 asks, *"Shall we continue in sin that grace may abound?"* No, because now we have authority over our flesh.

You actually could continue in sin and be ineffective—in constant pursuit of lies, a hamster on a wheel, more like Sisyphus in Greek mythology, the king of Corinth punished to push a boulder up a hill only to have it roll down, which he repeated throughout eternity. This is the lie of discord with GOD's order. The lie you are being told is that you are gaining a foothold on the desires of your heart—happiness, being accepted, looking good, being assertive—only to find out you've been rolling a boulder. You are putting in work that has no gain because it is contrary to the order of GOD. Man should be walking upright, advancing in his relationship with GOD and enjoying dominion over creation. He must get dominion over his actions by surrendering his heart to CHRIST first. He must get to know CHRIST and the promises of GOD as relayed in the Bible to come to this point.

So many people are carrying a god, are married to an idol, or are living in bondage, hoping that one day it will morph into freedom and wealth. In truth they are only deceiving themselves and others with a lie they try to mask, cover, and conceal trying to keep from going insane. The freedom of sanity is in walking in the order GOD established in his Word because it manifests the true fruit of the Spirit.

GOD can't be pimped or whored because He is the GOD of everything and can't be tempted to evil (James 1:13). That is to say, GOD can't be swayed by temptation to move against his Truth or his Word. I have folk say the Bible contradicts itself, specifically the matter of temptation with CHRIST being tempted or GOD being tempted. That act, or attempt, is the temptation of the mind of the FATHER towards the act is *not moved* by the act. (Trying to tempt is not tempting. The act is described with the word, not the affect.) They held grapes out to temp the stranger from his task, but he was unmoved. If GOD could be tempted, man would be GOD and use the Almighty like a genie.

Praise GOD Almighty for the order He has established because, in the faith of GOD and his Word, we should only fear *Him*. GOD is faithful and can't be tempted or moved by evil. He is GOD and established as sovereign by Himself. There is no greater power or authority that could ordain it. In this, we should worship GOD only and fear only GOD.

Chapter 4

FEAR, THE GREAT SEPARATOR

There are two types of fear I will deal with, even though there are scholars who say there are many more. There is the fear of the LORD, which is the only one we should embrace. Then, there is the fear that separates—the fear that separates and exalts others above GOD. We should fear GOD only, as nothing is greater. To fear is to doubt GOD; to doubt GOD means you do not have a right relationship with Him (to the detriment of yourself). GOD is all powerful, and He loves us. All that He has created is for our joy. 1 John 4:18 states, *"There is no fear in love; but perfect love casteth out fear: because fear hath torment, He that feareth is not made perfect in love."* GOD is perfect love and does not fear anything (because nothing is greater). His love for us (as realized in a right relationship) ensures us that we are kept by Him. By abiding in fear, we doubt the love of GOD and deny ourselves from truly embracing GOD and the creation He has made for our enjoyment.

Fear is the perfect prison. It is created by its captives and guarded by its prisoners. We are the wardens of the prison, as we can lock ourselves in it, yet can release ourselves at any time. The prison of fear is only in our minds. We have all heard the mnemonic for fear: False, Evidence, Appearing, Real. That is what fear is. Our Savior's murder was attempted at Golgotha (The Place of the Skull). He knew perfect love and was perfect love, and His faith raised Him from the dead. We are attacked in our minds, and our ability to survive the murder attempts is based on what we believe our lives are worth and to whom we believe our lives belong. Our lives are precious and have been bought by a Savior's blood.

The strategy of fear is to prompt us to search our vulnerabilities and accept all the things we are subject to that can harm or destroy us and live it. It does not matter that the attack is not real. We live and visualize the attacks that may or may not be real and respond as if they are real in the cell of our mind. We can't get free because we *live it bigger than the reality is*. Our tendency is to shun, blame, stereotype, and hate to make our fears real and justified. We are the wardens of our prisons, but prisons are prisons regardless of whether they are in the mind or real. They are intended to be restrictive. LOVE liberates, and perfect LOVE casts out fear. GOD is perfect LOVE, and He has no fear. We should only fear, or reverence, GOD.

There was a king in Israel, King Asa who had a heart to do what was right before the LORD. When the Ethiopians were assembling to conquer him, he prayed to the LORD:

Asa "prayed"

"*10 Then Asa went out against him, and they set the battle
in array in the valley of Zephathah at Mareshah.*
*11 And Asa cried unto the Lord his God, and said, Lord,
it is nothing with thee to help, whether with many,
or with them that have no power: help us, O Lord
our God; for we rest on thee, and in thy name we go
against this multitude. O Lord, thou art our God; let
no man prevail against thee*"

(2 Chronicle 14:10 – 11)

The prayer shows how he was completely dependent on the
LORD to save him, and the LORD answered his prayer and
defeated the Ethiopians and chased after them. (They ran from
him with greater numbers.) Yet, later, when Asa had another
army confront him, he didn't turn to the LORD, instead he made
a pact with another country. Why? Fear. In the first battle, he had
nowhere else to turn, and the LORD proved Himself faithful. In
the second battle, ASA had time to meditate on his own life and
faithfulness and made the power of the LORD a contingency
based on his doings. This meant that Asa had not judged *himself*
as faithful, so he doubted the LORD would answer his prayer,
so he did not ask.

Unlike David the King who, no matter what situation he was
in, would turn to the LORD for righteousness, for answers, and
for defense. Because, even though he sinned, his heart wanted to
be right before the LORD. He knew that without the fellowship

of the FATHER the kingship was merely a title. David knew he needed the power of the LORD with him. He loved the LORD, even though he knew he fell short often. He believed the LORD would correct him and not forsake him as Earthly fathers sometimes do. I have a son, Joshua, who I believe to be an amazing man, but he loses his way at times. But no matter what, he is mine, and I am here for him as long as he wants me to be. GOD ALMIGHTY loves us even more.

We often deem ourselves unworthy and are ashamed and refuse to go before the LORD (which is where the enemy wants you, alone in the wilderness so he can get in your head). We all do it. We self-judge and decide whether or not we believe the LORD will answer our prayers and decide not to even ask. Since Asa did not ask, he did not receive. Later he was rebuked and told that, since he did not ask, he would be at war for the rest of his life. He still didn't learn because he later was diseased in his feet and, instead of praying for healing, he went to the doctor. He was, yet again, reminded that the LORD had spoken a covenant to him, saying that He would be with him. He did not call on the LORD, and the foot disease killed him. There is nothing wrong with going to the doctor if GOD himself has not come and made a covenant with you and told you that you can call on Him and He will hear you. Wait! We all have that covenant, for those who believe as such as it is written in 1 John 5:13 – 20:

"13 These things have I written unto you that believe on the name of the Son of God; that ye may know that

ye have eternal life, and that ye may believe on the name of the Son of God.

14 *And this is the confidence that we have in him, that, if we ask anything according to his will, he heareth us:*

15 *And if we know that he hear us, whatsoever we ask, we know that we have the petitions that we desired of him.*

16 *If any man see his brother sin a sin which is not unto death, he shall ask, and he shall give him life for them that sin not unto death. There is a sin unto death: I do not say that he shall pray for it.*

17 *All unrighteousness is sin: and there is a sin not unto death.*

18 *We know that whosoever is born of God sinneth not; but he that is begotten of God keepeth himself, and that wicked one toucheth him not.*

19 *And we know that we are of God, and the whole world lieth in wickedness.*

20 *And we know that the Son of God is come, and hath given us an understanding, that we may know him that is true, and we are in him that is true, even in his Son Jesus Christ. This is the true God, and eternal life.*"

We have a relationship, through obedience, with the GOD of all things. He will hear and answer our prayers if we accept JESUS as LORD of our lives. We must follow His commandments and walk upright before Him. Not like He is some egotistical ruler demanding subservience, but because it is the order that GOD established for all things to live together. If we think we are nothing, or that GOD does not love us, we are reminded who we are in the LORD in Psalms 8: 3-9:

> "*3 When I consider thy heavens, the work of thy fingers, the moon and the stars, which thou hast ordained;*
>
> *4 What is man, that thou art mindful of him? and the son of man, that thou visitest him?*
>
> *5 For thou hast made him a little lower than the angels, and hast crowned him with glory and honour.*
>
> *6 Thou madest him to have dominion over the works of thy hands; thou hast put all things under his feet:*
>
> *7 All sheep and oxen, yea, and the beasts of the field;*
>
> *8 The fowl of the air, and the fish of the sea, and whatsoever passeth through the paths of the seas.*
>
> *9 O Lord our Lord, how excellent is thy name in all the earth!*"

GOD gave man dominion over creation, and when we are in right relationship (which means we operate in the system and manner GOD established for man), we have perfect fellowship with creation. When we are operating outside of the order GOD has established and are in self, we are in sin. Sin is in direct rebellion to GOD, which is often predicated on the fear of the negative type, the fear that separates.

The source and sole purpose of evil is to separate us from GOD and all He has for us. The unbelief in the fact that GOD loves you and will keep no good thing from you causes rebellion, which is what brought about the fall of Lucifer and Adam. The belief that harm will befall you, or that the LORD will keep something from you (and not wages of disobedience), is the negative fear that hinders the joy and peace, which is the power of the love of GOD in your life.

Fear has torment. You can't embrace GOD and his creation for you if you are afraid that either will harm you. Sin kills, steals, and destroys. Being out of the will of GOD places us in subjection to the wages of sin, which is death. You can't be a person of faith *and* fear. Wavering faith is fear and fear has torment.

Often times our faith requires testing to cast out fear. This is perfect LOVE at work. Often, we do not want to be tested, but would rather not see who we truly are in the LORD. Somehow we believe that, if we are not tested, we dwell in the lie that our lives will be prolonged. GOD chastens whom He loves (as stated by Paul). There is no need to fear the chastisement of the LORD. It is the love of a FATHER towards a son.

There is good fear. It is reverence and understanding that to abide in evil towards GOD or authority could have negative consequences. Let me explain it better like this: GOD is Almighty and has ways. His ways are higher than ours, as He created us. The reverence, fear, and trembling is honor, as He is the Creator of all things. He is the only thing we should fear, which is not warranted if we are walking upright. Fear is real, and often, in the Bible, folk are greeted with the salutation "fear not." That is to say you are not in danger at this moment, as I interpret it. The phrase "fear not" is used 365 times in the Bible (ME, 2015). That number matches the days in the year, which led me to believe it should be a daily mantra. This mantra should remind us to fear not, for the LORD is with us. It should also remind us to not fear anything that cannot destroy the body and the soul, which only GOD can do.

I had a coach in high school tell me, "There was no such thing as respect. Folk are just afraid of how people will treat them if they do not treat them in a favorable manner." That coach's belief was that there is no respect, only fear. I disagree. Years later, I realize the difference is fear has torment; respect, or honor, does not. I can have great joy for the opportunity to show kindness to someone I appreciate. That is respect (not to be confused with respect of person) and it has no torment, so it is not fear. I had another teacher in high school, Cynthia Smith, who was feared by a lot of students because she would fail you. She held students to a very high standard. I had great respect for her and tried to please her. There was no fear in this display. I held her in high esteem. I believed she cared for me and held me to a higher standard. This is an example of respect.

The respect I have for the LORD does not have torment, but it is joy and honor to know I am not the equal of GOD. And, I am reminded that I could be utterly destroyed by the Creator (justly so), but His love is here to ensure I have life and that I have it more abundantly. Our Savior CHRIST JESUS has sacrificed, through the order established and ransomed for sin, to ensure that abundant life. The HOLY SPIRIT indwells me to ensure that I am reminded of the sacrifice and to empower me to live in the order established.

The evil, fear, is the pernicious paralyzer that keeps us from enjoying the creation GOD meant for us to explore. It prevents us from seeing His greatness and his love made manifest for us. There are those who are fear mongers who attempt to capitalize on the lie that we are not good enough or that we are undeserving of what GOD gave us. The enemy came to kill, to steal, and to destroy; his tools are fear and lies. This plan is to keep us from walking in the dominion granted us and to have us as a mockery to GOD as our Creator.

I had a conversation once with mentor of mine who said "idolatry is not natural, it is spiritual sickness." He went on to explain how the idolaters on the other side of Jordan were faithful to their idols. Only the Israelites wanted to worship other gods and build temples to other gods. I gave this a lot of thought and wondered why this was so. We see it in the natural order of abuse and adultery, though. The man, knowing the woman is married, seeks to pull all he can from her as dominance over the other man. He wants to have her yield to him and give of the things her husband gave her, so he can secretly dominate both of them. He wants explicit sex and acts that demonstrate dominance, not love.

It was not enough that Solomon married women who worshipped other gods. They wanted temples to their gods, like he built his God. It is an indictment to his God and his belief. To announce to your god, your servant is not faithful to you, therefore you are not a powerful god. GOD showed Hosea what it is like to be faithful to a harlot because GOD was faithful to the harlot that was Israel. Idolatry is a sickness and a definite sign of malfunctioning.

We rebel against the good and godly order GOD has established, which is your rebellion against that which will empower you. These barriers to entry into dominion and the authority of walking after the Spirit manifest themselves in so many ways. I could fill a book alone with just naming examples but, in short, they are all meant to ensure there is separation between a person and perfect relationship with creation. These barriers of fear keep us from further solidifying a relationship with the Creator, who would empower us to enjoy the life GOD created for us. Now you might ask: why would someone rebel against the good and godly order GOD has established? Some folk do not believe the world is abundant and, if other folk have things, they will not have access. These folk create and use fear as a barrier, as agents of evil. Dr. Karl Albrecht breaks down fear into 5 types:

- Extinction (Ceasing to "be" or exist)
- Mutilation or Bodily Invasion
- Loss of Autonomy
- Separation, Abandonment, or Rejection
- Humiliation, Shame or Worthlessness (Albrecht, 2014)

In truth, there are only two types of fear, as I stated before—there is the fear and reverence for GOD and the fear that separates us from Him that exalts itself above us and has us fear or even praise creation over the Creator. Agents of evil set these mindsets in media and socialize them for profit to limit to mock man and his Creator.

The 'creation' of GOD becomes an idol of worship for these agents and denies the Creator through their evil doctrine. In the midst of this lie you surrender your authority and seek to be protected by folk and systems that have little regard for you or the Creator. Fear exists because people create these barriers for control and profit. In truth, GOD holds the heart of the king in his hand and turns it whichever way he wishes (Proverbs 21) or in favor of those who are seeking to overcome and walk upright before Him.

Sure, there has been evil that has been the pervasive manner in which societies have lived. Some of those empires are no more. I believe this is necessary to show forth the power of GOD and how he covers his saints and the sacrifice that is made in full rebellion to the evil in obedience to GOD against all odds. We can focus on the fears or the assaults or the victories. The focus can be on the path to Rome lit with burning Christians or the decapitations from the Mongol hordes to ISAL. Or, we can focus on folk who have been martyred in their stance that GOD is love and did not intend for us to live in fear and tyranny. The Word asks what good is a posted guard if GOD does not watch over the people. I'll go even further to assert that, if men stood up and were obedient to GOD despite the opportunity for selfish gain, there would be no evil society.

The Bible shows that Jeroboam caused Israel to sin because he was more interested in saving tax revenue and commerce in his town as oppose to folk going to Jerusalem to worship at the temple and staying. He built high places of worship in Dan and Bethel and recruited base folk to serve as priests (as cited in the book of Kings, chapter 12, written by the prophet Jeremiah). What if they said 'no'? What if the people acknowledged that this was not the way GOD said He was to be worshipped and they refused to go and worship at the high places? What if these folk, who knew they were not priests, had said 'no'? The fear of Jeroboam's wrath and greed caused folk to choose **hell** over GOD's righteousness, which removes them from the hedge of GOD and subsequent dearth and enslavement. The dearth and enslavement was GOD chastening Israel to turn them away from idols and back to Him, as only GOD has the perfect love that can sustain us. So evil is established as a system of operation in the world. Ezekiel 18:24 asserts;

> *"But when the righteous turneth away from his righteousness, and committeth iniquity, and doeth according to all the abominations that the wicked man doeth, shall he live? All his righteousness that he hath done shall not be mentioned; in his trespass that he hath trespassed, and in his sin that he hath sinned, in them shall he die."*

We have to decide who we will serve: sin and death <u>or</u> righteousness and life, as asked in Romans 6: 16 *"Know ye not, that to whom ye yield yourselves servant to obey, his servant ye are to whom ye obey; whether of sin unto death, or obedience unto righteousness?"* This speaks to the responsibility of the *individual* to resist sin and the *authority* we have to do so. The enemy is not more powerful than GOD, and GOD has given us power through the HOLY SPIRIT and the resurrected CHRIST to command our bodies and mind to live righteously. Fear is the agent used to convince us that this is not possible.

When the Word of GOD says, in 2 Corinthians 10:14, that, *"For the weapons of our warfare are not carnal, but mighty through God to the pulling down of strong holds."* This speaks directly to the spiritual power within us to tear down sin nature steeped in recidivism perpetuated as a curse. Praise GOD for the blood of CHRIST!

I love the stories of David, as GOD said he had found a man after his own heart (1 Samuel 13:14, and in Acts 13:22. This was possible because David was fearless before the LORD. David had faith that the LORD was with him and would strengthen him to be used to His glory. David did not fear the lion, the bear, Goliath, or any army, as he had faith in the LORD GOD ALMIGHTY. Faith is the necessity for casting out fear through love. The Word of GOD says it is impossible to please GOD without faith (Hebrews 11:6). We must read the Word of GOD to begin to walk in faith and to be liberated from the fear that separates us from Him and the creation He made for our joy. We have to decide to walk in faith.

Chapter 5

FAITH

Hebrews 11 King James Version (KJV)

"*1 Now faith is the substance of things hoped for, the evidence of things not seen.*

2 For by it the elders obtained a good report.

3 Through faith we understand that the worlds were framed by the word of God, so that things which are seen were not made of things which do appear.

4 By faith Abel offered unto God a more excellent sacrifice than Cain, by which he obtained witness that he was righteous, God testifying of his gifts: and by it he being dead yet speaketh.

5 By faith Enoch was translated that he should not see death; and was not found, because God had translated him: for before his translation he had this testimony, that he pleased God.

6 But without faith it is impossible to please him: for he that cometh to God must believe that he is, and that he is a rewarder of them that diligently seek him.

7 *By faith Noah, being warned of God of things not seen as yet, moved with fear, prepared an ark to the saving of his house; by the which he condemned the world, and became heir of the righteousness which is by faith.*

8 *By faith Abraham, when he was called to go out into a place which he should after receive for an inheritance, obeyed; and he went out, not knowing whither he went.*

9 *By faith he sojourned in the land of promise, as in a strange country, dwelling in tabernacles with Isaac and Jacob, the heirs with him of the same promise:*

10 *For he looked for a city which hath foundations, whose builder and maker is God.*

11 *Through faith also Sara herself received strength to conceive seed, and was delivered of a child when she was past age, because she judged him faithful who had promised.*

12 *Therefore sprang there even of one, and him as good as dead, so many as the stars of the sky in multitude, and as the sand which is by the sea shore innumerable.*

13 *These all died in faith, not having received the promises, but having seen them afar off, and were persuaded of them, and embraced them, and confessed that they were strangers and pilgrims on the earth.*

14 *For they that say such things declare plainly that they seek a country.*

15 *And truly, if they had been mindful of that country from whence they came out, they might have had opportunity to have returned.*

16 *But now they desire a better country, that is, an heavenly: wherefore God is not ashamed to be called their God: for he hath prepared for them a city.*

17 *By faith Abraham, when he was tried, offered up Isaac: and he that had received the promises offered up his only begotten son,*

18 *Of whom it was said, That in Isaac shall thy seed be called:*

19 *Accounting that God was able to raise him up, even from the dead; from whence also he received him in a figure.*

20 *By faith Isaac blessed Jacob and Esau concerning things to come.*

21 *By faith Jacob, when he was a dying, blessed both the sons of Joseph; and worshipped, leaning upon the top of his staff.*

22 *By faith Joseph, when he died, made mention of the departing of the children of Israel; and gave commandment concerning his bones.*

23 *By faith Moses, when he was born, was hid three months of his parents, because they saw he was a proper child; and they were not afraid of the king's commandment.*

24 *By faith Moses, when he was come to years, refused to be called the son of Pharaoh's daughter;*

25 *Choosing rather to suffer affliction with the people of God, than to enjoy the pleasures of sin for a season;*

26 *Esteeming the reproach of Christ greater riches than the treasures in Egypt: for he had respect unto the recompence of the reward.*

27 *By faith he forsook Egypt, not fearing the wrath of the king: for he endured, as seeing him who is invisible.*

28 *Through faith he kept the passover, and the sprinkling of blood, lest he that destroyed the firstborn should touch them.*

29 *By faith they passed through the Red sea as by dry land: which the Egyptians assaying to do were drowned.*

30 *By faith the walls of Jericho fell down, after they were compassed about seven days.*

31 *By faith the harlot Rahab perished not with them that believed not, when she had received the spies with peace.*

32 *And what shall I more say? for the time would fail me to tell of Gedeon, and of Barak, and of Samson, and of Jephthae; of David also, and Samuel, and of the prophets:*

33 *Who through faith subdued kingdoms, wrought righteousness, obtained promises, stopped the mouths of lions.*

34 *Quenched the violence of fire, escaped the edge of the sword, out of weakness were made strong, waxed*

valiant in fight, turned to flight the armies of the aliens.

35 Women received their dead raised to life again: and others were tortured, not accepting deliverance; that they might obtain a better resurrection:

36 And others had trial of cruel mockings and scourgings, yea, moreover of bonds and imprisonment:

37 They were stoned, they were sawn asunder, were tempted, were slain with the sword: they wandered about in sheepskins and goatskins; being destitute, afflicted, tormented;

38 (Of whom the world was not worthy:) they wandered in deserts, and in mountains, and in dens and caves of the earth.

39 And these all, having obtained a good report through faith, received not the promise:

40 God having provided some better thing for us, that they without us should not be made perfect."

I start out with this scripture on faith because the Word says without faith it is impossible to please GOD. So we need to understand what faith is and the power we gain with it. I also believe it is important to show examples of men (heroes of the faith) who walked courageously before the LORD seeking to please Him and to be in proper fellowship. Faith is the only thing that can conquer fear. Faith is the manner in which you assert and confirm your belief that GOD is Almighty and that you have surrendered to His order for salvation by accepting

JESUS CHRIST as your Savior. If that is not liberating and empowering for you, you need to be girded up and educated on what it means to be saved. Without faith it is impossible to please GOD, as faith represents buy in. I used to have a lot of problems with this, as I always wanted be an individual and stand alone. I viewed Christians as "sheople" (the words sheep and people combination), weak folk who needed a savior or a god to help them deal with their fears. I believed with a strong singular wit, a healthy bank account, and a good stiff left jab, a man could have anything he wanted if he was confident enough.

I didn't believe there was a need for GOD. Not that I minded Christians or their faith, but I saw it as an indicator of weakness and an opening to exploit their weaknesses and vulnerabilities. Even though I had accepted Christ as my Savior (in ritual of process), my heart was not transformed because I saw the hierarchy in the church. I saw a pastor or preacher who was living off the money of parishioners, filling them with guilt for not giving enough. Pastors were having sex with weak women or cunning women who were lost or desired things and his cronies who benefited from ensuring folk stayed in line so they all could "eat" (eat, slang for 'thrive').

I saw this in church after church. And, in the white churches I attended, the sex part may not have been as prolific, but the money part was. As I studied the Bible, I saw that this madness has existed since Jeroboam son of Nabat, and it has been perfected here. I also had to learn that this was not the church GOD intended, and it was weak in the power or authority needed to cultivate men of valor, men of strong faith. This system stripped men of faith as it had a form of godliness, yet it lacked the power thereof, as proclaimed in 2 Timothy 3: 1 – 7:

> "*1 This know also, that in the last days perilous times shall come.*
>
> *2 For men shall be lovers of their own selves, covetous, boasters, proud, blasphemers, disobedient to parents, unthankful, unholy,*
>
> *3 Without natural affection, trucebreakers, false accusers, incontinent, fierce, despisers of those that are good,*
>
> *4 Traitors, heady, highminded, lovers of pleasures more than lovers of God;*
>
> *5 Having a form of godliness, but denying the power thereof: from such turn away.*
>
> *6 For of this sort are they which creep into houses, and lead captive silly women laden with sins, led away with divers lusts,*
>
> *7 Ever learning, and never able to come to the knowledge of the truth.*"

This scripture perfectly described the nature of the church as I saw it, and I believed its practitioners and parishioners were ignorant, as they had not studied the Word for themselves. They were being led in a fashion that stripped them of their responsibility to keep the man, or pastor, honest. They could not call him out because they, not only did not know the Word other than what "pastor said," but the forum, or gathering that allowed for dialogue and correction, was nonexistent. These folk are denying themselves of the building blocks—the nourishment needed to have faith—and see it strengthened and grown. Where does faith come from? *"Faith commeth by hearing and hearing by the word of GOD"* (Romans 10:17).

There are those who will say that their pastor reads scripture in service. He might, but does he then go into a diatribe of describing what you heard and using text that has nothing to do with the situation? How many times have you heard Malachi 3 misused? The pastor, right before he takes an offering, will say *"Can a man rob GOD!?"* and the LORD says *"you have robbed me with your tithed gifts and offerings."* This is to make the parishioners consider all the things they did with God's money. They're thinking about the hot wings they bought, that bottle of whiskey, the new clothes, or whatever it is that is keeping them from believing they have that ten percent of their gross income they OWE God.

In context, the children of Israel were bringing to the priests diseased sheep and the worst and remnants of what they had as offerings because they had lost faith. They were weary from captivity and drought. GOD was establishing with them that He was still their GOD and that He was mindful of them. He was saying "let us break this cycle by giving me your best," and I will bless you abundantly. I believe this scripture is useful in showing how GOD will meet us in our obedience but not to guilt folk into believing they have robbed Him. That scripture is very situational, as many are, and easily misused for manipulation.

Want to know what perfect Church looks like? On the day of Pentecost when the HOLY SPIRIT filled men and they spoke in diverse tongues and were heard of each other in their own language. There were men who ridiculed and accused these men of drunkenness, yet their hearts were transformed once Peter spoke to them of the prophecy of Joel and of David. The Word says "their hearts were pricked," and they asked "What shall we do?" The Church was formed. These men immediately began to fellowship, sell their possessions, and give to each as they had need. They dined together in this fellowship and prayed for and with one another. They praised GOD and showed forth the love of GOD to all:

> "⁴¹ Then they that gladly received his word were baptized: and the same day there were added unto them about three thousand souls.
>
> ⁴² And they continued steadfastly in the apostles' doctrine and fellowship, and in breaking of bread, and in prayers.
>
> ⁴³ And fear came upon every soul: and many wonders and signs were done by the apostles.
>
> ⁴⁴ And all that believed were together, and had all things common;
>
> ⁴⁵ And sold their possessions and goods, and parted them to all men, as every man had need.
>
> ⁴⁶ And they, continuing daily with one accord in the temple, and breaking bread from house to house, did eat their meat with gladness and singleness of heart,

⁴⁷ *Praising God, and having favour with all the people. And the Lord added to the church daily such as should be saved."* (Acts 2:41–17)

The Word came forth, and faith was made manifest. With that faith came works. The Bible is clear that *"Faith without works is dead" (James 2:20 and 2:26).* There is a vast difference from this effective Church of Pentecost and the ineffective church of today that I compared to the church of Jeroboam son of Nabat (that caused Israel to sin). I make the comparison plain. The high places had fake priests, fake holidays to entertain the people, demands for offerings, makeshift temples, no HOLY SPIRIT, and no gospel truth spoken by a man of GOD.

The Pentecost Church was filled with the HOLY SPIRIT, and the Word of GOD was preached by a man who loved the LORD. Men *gave*, as opposed to taking, and *were saved*, as opposed to being pacified and sent home. Faith is built where the Word is studied, preached, discussed, and shared. It is hard to build strong Christians filled with the HOLY SPIRIT and doing the will of GOD when they are only in the Word for a couple of hours (if that) once or twice per week, attending the "church show" and, having limited interactions with Saints who are seeking to do GOD's will.

Faith is power to overcome sin. Activate in yourself the power of the HOLY SPIRIT through the use of his full armor, so you can fight the good fight and celebrate creation. If you don't know who your enemy is and you're not getting clear direction and instruction from the Bible (the life guide user's manual), how can you know what you are, whose you are, and what to do? If you don't know these things, you are not studying your Bible. Sound doctrine breeds sound Christians who are indomitable and loving. There are many people, devices, and systems hell bent on your demise, more so your compliance and inactivity, to the end of robbing you of your birth right (dominion) and to use you for profit.

The great thing about faith is that, when you have done all you can or know to do, when there seems to be nowhere else to go, GOD is there. There is no bottom. The options are not exhausted as *"the king's heart is in the hand of the Lord, as the rivers of water: he turneth it whithersoever he will" (Proverbs 21:1).* The oil cup does not fail—water is turned to wine, men run across deserts, the few defeat the many, the dead are awaken, and the sick are healed. There is no condition the LORD can't change, reprise, or correct for the faithful.

There are levels of faith. Some are fine with receiving food, others are healed, while some expect and pray for demons to be cast out, and the laws of physics are broken. The LORD has said *"According to your faith be it to you" (Matthew 9:29).* When it comes to the unsaved centurion, Jesus marveled at his faith and commented that He had not seen such faith in Israel. What was so special about the centurion's faith? The centurion was able to develop faith from watching order and nature to establish at the utterance of the Word. Real faith. CHRIST is the Word made flesh. All of creation speaks to the order of GOD and the power of overcoming adversity.

Ever see a root break through concrete? Ever watch an animal escape a group of attackers that looked like certain death? How does a tree grow from a seed, or animals survive perilous journeys to spawning grounds? These are testaments to the power of will. Imagine what happens when you add faith and promise to a will to serve GOD. With understanding of who you are in creation and what you mean to your FATHER in heaven there is real power there. This is precious for those who have accepted CHRIST as their Savior and are committed to walking after the Spirit and not after the flesh.

Faith has meant so much to me. I can't begin to explain how I live it at every minute of my life, as I have known GOD's grace and mercy. I have had the LORD manifest such compassion when I was at my wits end and sustain me beyond my last dollar and to the end of my resources. I have had checks come in the mail unexpectedly from money I didn't know I had. Cars donated to me, clothes purchased, tuitions paid, debts forgiven, storms pass over, cars go beyond tank limitations, healings in my body, jobs, businesses, prayers answered, and favor given to me and my family. I could go on and on about all that GOD has manifested after I had given all I had, or had nothing but prayer left. And GOD showed up!

The work part of the faith process is as essential to the outcome because the work part legitimizes the request. Imagine Moses standing on a hill with his arms up to the point where other folk had to help hold them up, to finally having to get a stones for him to sit on. But, he endured. Then Joshua defeated the Amalek because faith and work were combined, as Moses prevailed and his arms remained up. Imagine Peter getting out of the boat to even attempt to walk on water at the beckoning of the LORD. We concentrate on the fact that his faith was not strong enough to keep him held up, but he got out the boat and took steps. That's faith and effort!

I have to restate, again, that GOD is not a genie. Prayers and wishes are not the same. Prayers are predicated on biblical principles and the order GOD has created and not on lusts. Faith does not make life perfect or ensure that you get everything you want. What faith does is provide you with the evidence you can hope for. Peter saw Jesus walking on water (evidence it could be done) and hoped he could do it as well. He stepped out (doing the work), and his faith held up until he doubted. *"Faith is the substance of thing hoped for, the evidence of things not seen" (Hebrews 11:1)*. Faith comes from the Word, proof of an Almighty GOD who loves man and is mindful of him.

The Bible is proof that GOD can, and has, made a way out of no way. The Word demonstrates that, as Paul said in the Word, *"I can do all things through Christ which strengthenth me"(Philippians 4:13)*. Paul's confession was to acknowledge the many trials he had suffered, and he was confessing his faith in the LORD to strengthen him and keep him in any situation. Faith does not mean there are no trials. Trials are there to prove and strengthen your faith. The conclusion you should hope for is made manifest through the Word of GOD. Your knowledge of the Word will increase and feed your faith so hope is not lost. This would assure you that you will work until your faith brings what you hope for into fruition. Romans 15:4 (KJV) explains that, *"⁴ For whatsoever things were written aforetime were written for our learning, that we through patience and comfort of the scriptures might have hope."* The knowledge of the Word and the relationship with the FATHER through CHRIST JESUS, the Redeemer, while being filled with the HOLY GHOST pleases GOD as in Ephesians 5:14 –21:

> "*14 Wherefore he saith, Awake thou that sleepest, and arise from the dead, and Christ shall give thee light.*
>
> *15 See then that ye walk circumspectly, not as fools, but as wise,*
>
> *16 Redeeming the time, because the days are evil.*
>
> *17 Wherefore be ye not unwise, but understanding what the will of the Lord is.*
>
> *18 And be not drunk with wine, wherein is excess; but be filled with the Spirit;*
>
> *19 Speaking to yourselves in psalms and hymns and spiritual songs, singing and making melody in your heart to the Lord;*
>
> *20 Giving thanks always for all things unto God and the Father in the name of our Lord Jesus Christ;*
>
> *21 Submitting yourselves one to another in the fear of God.*"

This scripture encourages the reader to "wake up"—to no longer be unaware, to take action, and to understand there is evil. Jesus will give you a pathway to righteousness. You must understand it is not time to drink yourself to forgetfulness or to go party and behave as if there is no fight. We are instructed to walk after the

Spirit, pray, and praise GOD, giving thanks for the Savior. The way to be saved is to submit to these ways and commandments. This walk is serious, and it should not look like the world, as it is an endeavor of faith and works bringing forth the things hoped for from the unseen.

The walk of faith becomes difficult, as folk tend to lose focus and concentration because there are so many distractions and so much noise. The scripture with Peter walking on water is one I love as a demonstration of faith because it illustrates faith cometh by hearing and hearing by the Word of GOD. (Jesus is the Word, and He bid Peter come.) Faith is the substance of things hoped for, the evidence of things unseen. Peter had faith manifest when he had heard the Word of GOD (CHRIST) and had hope that he could obey and "come" to JESUS by walking on water. It was something he had not seen for himself or done, yet he hoped for it. (Faith without works is dead.) So Peter stepped out the boat (the work of faith) and walked on water, demonstrating faithfulness to the Word. Peter sank because he listened to the noise that was contrary to the Word given. He believed the noise from the wind and surf, or information contrary to the Word, to be more powerful to him than the Word that beckoned him to "come". Here is the scripture:

> "26 And when the disciples saw him walking on the sea, they were troubled, saying, It is a spirit; and they cried out for fear.
> 27 But straightway Jesus spake unto them, saying, Be of good cheer; it is I; be not afraid.

28 *And Peter answered him and said, Lord, if it be thou, bid me come unto thee on the water.*

29 *And he said, Come. And when Peter was come down out of the ship, he walked on the water, to go to Jesus.*

30 *But when he saw the wind boisterous, he was afraid; and beginning to sink, he cried, saying, Lord, save me.*

31 *And immediately Jesus stretched forth his hand, and caught him, and said unto him, O thou of little faith, wherefore didst thou doubt?*

32 *And when they were come into the ship, the wind ceased.*

33 *Then they that were in the ship came and worshipped him, saying, Of a truth thou art the Son of God."*

(Matthew 14:26, KJV)

We have to establish faithfulness in our lives for our faith to be effective. Faithfulness is where we decide that the object of our faith is Truth—the only Truth. This Truth renders noise ineffective. If Peter had not made the wind and the waves lord over JESUS, he would not have begun to sink, but he doubted (which is to remove the power and not remain faithful) the Word.

Agathocles of Syracuse in 310 BC, Emperor Julian in 363, William of Normandy in 1066, and Cortez in 1519; all burned their ships after the troops arrived for battle so there would be no means for retreat (Sledge, 2017). Faithfulness is a matter of "burning the ships" in your mind (fear, doubt, escape routes, other options). There is no retreat, no other action available.

Imagine how the divorce rate would drop if, after marriage, there were no other options. What I mean is, if there were no way to cheat with anyone else or to be comforted by anyone else—if the husband or wife you choose was the only answer for marital bliss. Married folk would have to find a way to live together, because who wants to spend the rest of their lives miserable? Now, even if they do not have extramarital affairs, their lives are filled with retreats—TV the company of others, work, the kids, everything else but hammering out the issues and dedicating themselves to ensuring the marriage lines up with the Word of GOD. Marriage takes faith. It is a symbol of the covenant relationship between the Church and CHRIST. We are saved by CHRIST through faith.

Solomon, after building the temple to GOD, asked GOD to be faithful to him. He asked GOD to be merciful. If men turned and prayed towards the temple, he asked GOD to remember them. Solomon lacked faithfulness. He had faith that GOD was GOD, yet he was unfaithful. Over time he built altars to other gods. He listened to the noise from all the women he had and sought to please them. He was not focused on the Word as the only truth.

Like Peter and Solomon, most folk who fail to walk upright after hearing the Word begin to listen to the noise and give in to hearts that are unfaithful, filled with lusts, desires, and fears. We often decide that, because we do not want to do the work, there must be another answer—an easier way, so we create other truths or realities. In truth, the boats are always burned. There is no alternative. Our retreats are an illusion, a distraction from the inevitable. There is only one GOD, and JESUS is the only way to salvation. Everything else is an illusion. All other worship and actions lead to death as are the wages of sin. Disobedience to GOD is sin. This is no joke. It is a fight for your eternal soul, and it is the way to eternal joy through righteous living. It is difficult. Righteous living can be hard because the path is filled with liars, naysayers, and temptation. But, if we burn the ships and move forward only towards the victory in CHRIST JESUS, we will find life more abundant.

There is a cross on a hill with a blood-stained banner in the vision of most saints who believe that JESUS suffered on the cross and died for their sins. He is now sitting at the right hand of POWER praying for them that they may have life and have it more abundantly. This is why the Word of GOD is so important for establishing faith because it speaks of the rewards of the war and righteous living.

The Bible attempts to explain it in a fashion we can receive with passages that speak to mansions, crowns, treasure and everlasting joy, but we have to understand what GOD created here is corruptible. What He has for saints in heaven is not. Our life's work is to accept CHRIST JESUS as Savior for redemption of sin and to have fellowship with the Creator and his creation in the order GOD has established. That looks like walking after the Spirit, which yields fruit and peace, and then there is an award ceremony and eternal joy and peace.

If your life is filled with the wages of fleshly living, it is because you are not walking after the Spirit. That is not a judgment. It is a biblical Truth. Sure there are trials and tribulation, but the heart of a man speaks to where he lives and to what he or she believes. The value of a man and the quality of life is not established by external forces and people; it is a choice. Faith is the catalyst that determines the value of a man's life, and it is demonstrated by faithful living.

Noise from fake life on television does not operate in the order GOD has established. It lies and distorts expectations, as it is contrived and does not follow the order GOD has created naturally. Every life event won't take thirty minutes to resolve and won't always end happily. The hero does not always get the girl, and sometimes things are not fair. The truth of the matter is you should be encouraged by the Word of GOD and through the testimonies of other saints. This builds faith and gives us the hope we need to put works into actions that bear fruit. Noise from other sources can cause doubt and also move us away from sources that encourage, as most often noise is time-consuming and hard to bear, since it is also contrary to GOD's established order.

Chapter 6

NOISE

"**I**n the beginning was the Word, and the Word was with God, and the Word was God" (John 1:1). The Word is the order GOD established for creation. The Word speaks to the relationship between GOD and creation. Order is established, and outcomes and effects of all actions, are in the order established by the Creator. We can learn the Word, have a relationship with the Word (good or bad), obey the Word, or ignore the Word. The actions we take will have outcomes that will determine how creation interacts with us. Currently, folk are calling this order "the universe," and celebrating the creation above the Creator. (This is a great example of noise.) As order is established by the Creator, the creation merely responds to the order established by the Creator to the creation. Folk speaking of the universe doing thus and so rarely understand that the order of things is established by GOD the Creator.

The confluence of rhetoric establishing the independent consciousness of creation is a lie—noise established to justify desire and intent. We create false realities and use responses out of context to justify our beliefs and desires to empower our frailties and evade the Truth and its healing power. Beliefs that are contrary to the Word and that empower "things, thoughts, images" over the order GOD has created is noise. There are forces acting outside of the will of GOD that hope to have results contrary to the order that GOD has established. It will not happen as GOD has already ruled on the matter, they are in rebellion.

Rebellion is the propensity or action to move against the will of GOD, intentionally. My brother and I often discuss the first rebellion, the nature of it, and its effect on the noise we are subjected to today. As taught in the church, the enemy rebelled after being appointed over the praise and worship service and decided he was glorious and should rule. We were taught that the enemy and rebelling angels were cast out of heaven to the earth. We know that the enemy is the great accuser of man, and he has an audience with GOD where he accuses the creation to the Creator,

> *"And I heard a loud voice saying in heaven, Now is come salvation, and strength, and the kingdom of our God, and the power of his Christ: for the accuser of our brethren is cast down, which accused them before our God day and night."* (Revelations 12:10)

We see also in the book of Genesis the first example of noise caused by rebellion, as the enemy accuses GOD of lying to Adam and Eve when he says,

"⁴ And the serpent said unto the woman, Ye shall not surely die:

⁵ *For God doth know that in the day ye eat thereof, then your eyes shall be opened, and ye shall be as gods, knowing good and evil."* (Genesis 3:4 –5)

The message from the enemy (in the guise of a serpent) is in direct conflict with what GOD has said. It is contrived to have a man look for evidence that GOD is a liar. We have to know that GOD is not a man that He should lie (Numbers 23:19). We have to also accept that the Word of GOD is the Truth. Only in this can we began to filter out noise and decide to live by these Truths and accept them as the standard of life.

We will always have the excuse of blame and accusation from others (which are the tools of the enemy) as having an effect on the life we live and the choices we make. Often we are quick to say 'he or she made me angry, or caused me to sin,' based on their words or actions. We choose to sin or operate in a manner contrary to the results we want because we listen to noise. The Truth is our peace and joy is established by forces that are incorruptible. This is our strength, for the gifts and calling of GOD are without repentance (Romans 11:29).

JESUS did not sin, as He was the Word made flesh, and the Word is incorruptible and so is Truth. When we are saved and the HOLY SPIRIT, that indwells saints (those confessing CHRIST as Savior) and knows all things and empowers us. It gives us insight into the order GOD has established. All of creation submits to the order of the Creator, even if not to his will (which is rebellion and has negative consequences). The choices we make control the realities we live based on fleshly or spiritual walks (choices). We know what choices we have made beforehand by the Spirit that indwells us. We are sure by the manifestations or results of those choices as to whether they were spiritual or fleshly. The distortion between the intention and action that causes rebellion in choices contrary to the Spirit is noise. It is a small gap, but it is where the distortion, or lie, is planted.

> *"For the Word of God is quick and powerful and sharper than any two edged sword, piercing even to the dividing asunder of soul and spirit, and of the joints and marrow, and is a discerner of the thoughts and intents of the heart."* (Hebrew 4:12)

This scripture is powerful because it proves there is hope—hope from the Word to fight in the minutia between the heart, thoughts, intentions, and actions. We have to be mindful and obedient. The choice to be obedient to the Word, and line up with GOD's order, is the gift of free will. You go to church or read the Word. It resonates with you, and you decide to be mindful in that area of your life. For example, you hear the scripture:

> *"11 Speak not evil one of another, brethren. He that speaketh evil of his brother, and judgeth his brother, speaketh evil of the law, and judgeth the law: but if*

thou judge the law, thou art not a doer of the law, but a judge."

[12] *There is one lawgiver, who is able to save and to destroy: who art thou that judgest another?"*

(James 4:11–12)

You decide to extend grace to people and not be so quick to judge and condemn folk. Then, on the way home from work someone cuts you off, or you receive bad or rude service at the restaurant after church, and the scripture goes out the window. Why? Because this is real life, and that was church. You have a choice, but you have not decided that you do not have the right to control someone else's actions. You can control <u>you</u>. We have not extended the grace and mercy we have received to others. The Word is not real because we are listening to the noise to appease self.

The noise is all the words you hear that are contrary to the scripture, and they are opinions you have formed up to hearing that Word today. That person that cut you off in that car is not a person anymore. He is an idiot who is inconsiderate and cares only for his personal situation. In your mind, he does not deserve grace because he is not giving it. This is a lie—noise. That person giving you rude customer service at the restaurant is not a person, but an entitled dummy that should be happy someone at least let them wait tables. They are missing out on tips because they have no proper home training, and we decide that we are going to fix her by leaving a terrible tip and filling out the comment card (instead of showing love and possible some tutelage on what good service looks like). Matthew 5:13 (KJV) reminds us that, "*Ye are the salt of the earth: but if the salt have lost his savor, wherewith shall it be salted? It is thenceforth good for nothing, but to be cast out, and to be trodden under foot of men.*" We have to tune into the message and tune out the noise so we will be salt and light to the lost, and not worthless.

We have the goal set before us to be the best we can be, and we have the tools to be serious about the choices we make. The HOLY SPIRIT will guide you and ensure that you know what to do. The Word of GOD, the full armor, and faith will ensure you have the power to do what is needed of you. You are never alone, but the decisions and the work are yours to do.

The noise is unrelenting. It is warfare. In relation to communication, noise is anything that distracts from the message or its hearing. Standing on a factory floor yelling instructions is hard because of all the noise. It is also anything that keeps you from receiving from the Word of GOD. How do we hear from GOD, receive his Word, and walk upright through all the noise? It is done through dedication. It is deliberate. Walking upright is hard to do, though, if you are listening to garbage on the radio and watching hell on TV. It is distracting and divisive.

I can recall being on the flight line with aircraft engines running, people were everywhere, and everyone had a heightened sense of their surroundings. The message was clear: that if you were not dedicated to understanding your surroundings and what was expected of you, you could die. You can be around noise <u>and</u> be focused, "*be in this world not of it.*" *(Romans 12:2).* The fight is the same. The enemy is seeking to destroy you and to keep you from walking in the glory and birthright given you by the Creator. The noise blasted at you from many sources has one purpose alone: to cause us a slow agonizing death by our own hands, thereby proving us unworthy and unfit (the accusation of the enemy to the Creator regarding the creation). We already know we are unworthy and unfit, yet our Creator loves us and has bestowed upon us the opportunity to fellowship with Him and have dominion over creation in love. The question is: Will you listen to and abide by the Word of GOD, or will you listen to the noise broadcasted by the enemy?

Ephesians 2:2 explains, *"Wherein in time past ye walked according to the course of this world, according to the prince of the power of the air, the spirit that now worketh in the children of disobedience."* One of my pastors used to say it is "the prince and power of the air waves," as he believed the noise that was influencing the saints was from the TV and radio more so than from the Bible.

I agree and believe that disobedience is a result of rebellion manufactured through noise from media leading many to believe that GOD is unjust, that GOD is not essential to living, and that GOD is contrived by man to handle his fear and ignorance. And furthermore, it often leads man to believe *he* is GOD, and *he* gets to pick his higher power and its limitations (just like the Israelites' bid to Aaron). This is apparent when we listen to the noise, and it tells you its intentions boldly (to kill, to steal, and destroy, John 10:10). There are ways GOD has established that bring about the fruit of the Spirit, and there are ways that bring about the wages of sin. Man pursues the ways of the flesh, justifies the latter and lies about the results.

I often listen to arguments over liberalism and conservatism, and I have heard folk say the greatest assault on America is the rise of socialism by the liberal agenda. Then, I listen to another position that asserts the greatest threat to America is corporations, special interests, and the diminishing middle class. Then there is CNN and FOX News furthering the rift with cries about the reality of the news. In truth, they're all lying or rather holding back the truth. The Truth is the Word of GOD and the order He has established for living. It asks that we love each other and give of our lives that another may live. It is not our place to enforce limits on anyone and judge them based on any forum or position. I will give you Romans 14 and then come back this argument:

"1 Him that is weak in the faith receive ye, but not to doubtful disputations.

2 For one believeth that he may eat all things: another, who is weak, eateth herbs.

3 Let not him that eateth despise him that eateth not; and let not him which eateth not judge him that eateth: for God hath received him.

4 Who art thou that judgest another man's servant? to his own master he standeth or falleth. Yea, he shall be holden up: for God is able to make him stand.

5 One man esteemeth one day above another: another esteemeth every day alike. Let every man be fully persuaded in his own mind.

6 He that regardeth the day, regardeth it unto the Lord; and he that regardeth not the day, to the Lord he doth not regard it. He that eateth, eateth to the Lord, for he giveth God thanks; and he that eateth not, to the Lord he eateth not, and giveth God thanks.

7 For none of us liveth to himself, and no man dieth to himself.

8 For whether we live, we live unto the Lord; and whether we die, we die unto the Lord: whether we live therefore, or die, we are the Lord's.

9 For to this end Christ both died, and rose, and revived, that he might be Lord both of the dead and living.

10 But why dost thou judge thy brother? or why dost thou set at nought thy brother? for we shall all stand before the judgment seat of Christ.

11 For it is written, As I live, saith the Lord, every knee shall bow to me, and every tongue shall confess to God.

12 So then every one of us shall give account of himself to God.

13 Let us not therefore judge one another anymore: but judge this rather, that no man put a stumbling block or an occasion to fall in his brother's way.

14 I know, and am persuaded by the Lord Jesus, that there is nothing unclean of itself: but to him that esteemeth any thing to be unclean, to him it is unclean.

15 But if thy brother be grieved with thy meat, now walkest thou not charitably. Destroy not him with thy meat, for whom Christ died.

16 Let not then your good be evil spoken of:

17 For the kingdom of God is not meat and drink; but righteousness, and peace, and joy in the Holy Ghost.

18 For he that in these things serveth Christ is acceptable to God, and approved of men.

19 Let us therefore follow after the things which make for peace, and things wherewith one may edify another.

20 For meat destroy not the work of God. All things indeed are pure; but it is evil for that man who eateth with offence.

21 It is good neither to eat flesh, nor to drink wine, nor any thing whereby thy brother stumbleth, or is offended, or is made weak.

22 Hast thou faith? have it to thyself before God. Happy is he that condemneth not himself in that thing which he alloweth.

23 And he that doubteth is damned if he eat, because he eateth not of faith: for whatsoever is not of faith is sin." (Romans 14, KJV)

In reading this, what I get is that the things that make us different are less important than the GOD that connects us. What I understand is that every man will have to give an account for the choices he has made. The more relevant thing that I comprehend is that we assign dispositions and nomenclatures to each other so we can deny GOD's order for all men. We are missing the fellowship and power of unity sighting differences that GOD will settle at Judgment. On the issues GOD has already ruled on through the commandments, we need not argue these. What *we* do is create issues whereby we attempt to determine who is even human or born into a place to receive the dominion from GOD or to even the rights granted in the constitution. Once those issues were resolved, we created laws that ensured people's rights are not violated, seeking to have some semblance of civility. These laws ensure, or are supposed to, prohibit discrimination based on race, color, sex, religion, national origin, age, disability, and genetic information, as well as reprisal for protected activity (EEOC, 2018).

When these issues were resolved we began to turn each other into threats, creating hysteria and the broadcast noise become louder. We further justify hate, greed, and fear to fulfill our lusts by crying danger from hippies, invaders, gang members, free riders, and many other words to justify that there are spooky people hell bent on our destruction and the compromise of our way of living.

We are here to love each other. That's how we overcome and make it all better. There are people who want to love you, whom you have decided are incapable of loving you because you believe the noise, which states that only "your kind" can love you. "Love is at the root of everything. All learning, all parenting, all relationships. Love, or the lack of it." (Fred Rogers, "Mr. Rogers's Neighborhood").

What I love about my HEAVENLY FATHER is that He made variety. He created many peoples, flavors, and visions because we process information differently, quickly, and get bored easily. There a is rich calming in the depths of sound for me. I like vibrations, frequencies, interacting, and building music (sound stages). Music is of GOD. I see us all as his orchestration—rich and full, completely dependent to finish the work (a matter of my muse or vision). The noise of hate seeks to destroy the harmonious orchestration of love, which is in us all to share with each other as GOD's creations. It is more than intentions, but it is there. Many of us refuse to walk in it. This brings me to why there is death. The wages of sin is death—the rebellion of Truth and love.

Chapter 7

DEATH

Noise can kill you or provoke GOD to kill you or to have you killed. It may sound harsh, but GOD created you, and He has every authority (which is GOD's) to destroy what He has created. As GOD is a loving GOD, He established order for living and a way by which man could have the fruit of the Spirit in walking in obedience. I will remind you what the fruit of the Spirit is: *"love, joy, peace, longsuffering, gentleness, goodness, faith, 23 Meekness, temperance: against such there is no law" (Galatians 5:22 – 23).* This is the manifestation "The Fruit" of walking in GOD's order, and it is available to everyone without discrimination. Those who refuse to walk after the Spirit but after the flesh (meaning they have made a conscious effort in their hearts to be in rebellion) will reap the fruit of the flesh which is:

> *"19 Adultery, fornication, uncleanness, lasciviousness,*
> *20 Idolatry, witchcraft, hatred, variance, emulations, wrath, strife, seditions, heresies,*
> *21 Envyings, murders, drunkenness, revellings, and such like: of the which I tell you before, as I have also*

told you in time past, that they which do such things shall not inherit the kingdom of God."
(Galatians 5:20–21, KJV)

When these things are in a person's life, they are a direct reflection of the choices one has made, and he or she will be given the opportunity to hear the Word of GOD, be cleansed, and repent. Most are so weary, as the sole purpose of these life choices is to kill them with a slow, agonizing death. In most cases, these folk don't even know they are dying; they are just broken. When approached with light and salt in the hour of despair, most will run to the Cross—to the love of GOD—and be healed, transformed, and on fire for the LORD. I love these types of saints because they have been *through* it, and they are not disillusioned. They know there is nothing off the ark but death, so they cling. If they are nurtured in the Word and loved, they become mighty in the Lord. They die to self and the flesh, and they know it is the first death and resurrection of the Spirit which will bear fruit. The greatest love story of all is to be cleansed by the blood of JESUS and to be forgiven of sin and offered a chance to enjoy the order and creation of GOD in peace.

Then there are those—the stiff-necked and the hard-hearted—who have decided to embrace the noise and seek different solutions. The order of flesh in them is seeking power, glory, and sex, filled with vanity, as Solomon said there is only vanity for those who are seeking life outside of GOD's order. Some are given to reprobate minds because they are stiff-necked and hard-hearted, and eventually the wages of sin is death.

I have been asked how could a benevolent GOD kill people or allow the Israelites to kill other people or order the slaughter of folk. The wages of sin is death. It is the order GOD established because the willful disobedience to GOD's order erodes, kills, and destroys whatever comes against it. Disobedience is friction and erosion against GOD's order, which will never be triumphed over. This disobedience is in conflict and will dissipate or disintegrate through contact. The process of being in conflict with GOD also serves as an irritation or countering force to the righteous or those traveling in the right direction. If disobedience fails to yield, it will be destroyed.

There is good and evil. There is that which goes with righteousness, which is the order GOD created for man to have right relationship with creation. Then there is evil, or that which is brought about to kill man, steal his gift of dominion, and destroy the creation he has dominion over and is intended for man to enjoy. There is opportunity when there is conflict in this area, depending on how great that one force will subsides the other. There are many folk who have decided to be Christians (Disciples of CHRIST) from all walks of life, and there is grace to conform and flow in the order of creation. Then there are those who have willfully decided not to do so, and their destiny is both a physical and spiritual death. It is not a game. I knew a preacher who would say, before GOD allowed the enemy to have more souls, He would turn rocks into souls. (Can't find it in the Bible, though.) The matter becomes one of how long and how much one tolerates. GOD judges because he does not just allow folk to be justified in wrongdoing.

It was apparent when the Israelites crossed Jordan that the GOD of Abraham had been there before them. Balaam received messengers from the King of Moab. The king requested that Balaam speak to GOD and bid GOD to destroy the Israelites. GOD would speak with him (Balaam), and He said for them to leave the Israelites alone for they were blessed. The intention of the king of the Moabites was to wipe them from the earth. These people on the other side of Jordan, after having heard the Word of GOD and denying the GOD of creation, created their own gods. Some even patterned their religion after the promises and prophecies given to the Israelites to make it seem as if their gods were GOD.

There are several pagan religions that tell of a virgin birth and a savior, yet there is only one CHRIST. They can do this because they heard the Word, had an experience with GOD, and refused Him. Job was not a Hebrew. He was from Uz, yet he knew the rituals and processes known to Hebrew priests for praying to and worshipping GOD. He believed in GOD ALMIGHTY, but there were other folk who knew the GOD of creation, and had willfully turned away, and decided to kill the folk who had chosen to walk with GOD as his people. These pagan religions consisted of rituals involving sacrificing children, self-mutilation, and other forms of lascivious behavior. It was apparent that living with Moabites was not an option, as the influence of their evil could influence GOD's people. Balaam told those seeking to destroy the Israelites that warring with them was not the solution, but inter-marrying would be their downfall.

We can see time and again even with Solomon, the wisest man alive, that after building a temple to GOD, he shortly thereafter built temples to other gods and sacrificed his children to those other gods. There is no satisfying flesh; evil is all consuming. Only GOD can pass judgment to kill because only GOD can create. GOD is merciful, but in life there are occasions where the evil must be abolished to preserve the righteous. A man can't judge GOD. He sets the order and has made provisions for us to enjoy creation, yet the Word is clear that the thief comes but to kill, to steal, and to destroy (John 10:10). GOD is the defender of those He loves and of his order:

> *"But let all those that put their trust in thee rejoice: let them ever shout for joy, because thou defendest them: let them also that love thy name be joyful in thee."*   (Psalm 5:11)
>
> *"The Lord hears thee in the day of trouble; the name of the God of Jacob defend thee;Deliver me from mine enemies, O my God: defend me from them that rise up against me."*   (Psalm 20:1)
>
> *"Defend the poor and fatherless: do justice to the afflicted and needy."*   (Psalm 82:3)
>
> *"As birds flying, so will the Lord of hosts defend Jerusalem; defending also he will deliver it; and passing over he will preserve it."*   (Isaiah 31:5)

Defending the faithful and weak Christian against the tyranny of evil is an essential part of the relationship we have with the

LORD. Destruction of others is for GOD ALMIGHTY alone and his appointed. Destruction is not for folk claiming to be the left hand of GOD, or people who are angry and fearful of others based on race and or socio-economic status. If you have not heard from GOD directly, then killing other folk is not a task that is appointed you. I do understand, however, that freedom is not free and soldiers follow orders. One of my favorite movies is Sergeant York, and I believe that sometimes it is necessary to take life to ensure the innocent and weak may live. The LORD has ordered entire people killed—children, women, livestock, everything—and, on those occasions, GOD's appointed heard from Him or his prophet. If you are commanding a soldier to kill, you need to be sure you have heard from GOD. Ultimately, we war and kill each other because of lusts and sin. Sometimes the lust of a collective will grow to the point where they infringe upon the peace of others to satiate their desire. Take a look at James 4:1–12:

> "1 From whence come wars and fightings among you? come they not hence, even of your lusts that war in your members?
>
> 2 Ye lust, and have not: ye kill, and desire to have, and cannot obtain: ye fight and war, yet ye have not, because ye ask not.
>
> 3 Ye ask, and receive not, because ye ask amiss, that ye may consume it upon your lusts.
>
> 4 Ye adulterers and adulteresses, know ye not that the friendship of the world is enmity with God?

whosoever therefore will be a friend of the world is the enemy of God.

5 *Do ye think that the scripture saith in vain, The spirit that dwelleth in us lusteth to envy?*

6 *But he giveth more grace. Wherefore he saith, God resisteth the proud, but giveth grace unto the humble.*

7 *Submit yourselves therefore to God. Resist the devil, and he will flee from you.*

8 *Draw nigh to God, and he will draw nigh to you. Cleanse your hands, ye sinners; and purify your hearts, ye double minded.*

9 *Be afflicted, and mourn, and weep: let your laughter be turned to mourning, and your joy to heaviness.*

10 *Humble yourselves in the sight of the Lord, and he shall lift you up.*

11 *Speak not evil one of another, brethren. He that speaketh evil of his brother, and judgeth his brother, speaketh evil of the law, and judgeth the law: but if thou judge the law, thou art not a doer of the law, but a judge.*

12 *There is one lawgiver, who is able to save and to destroy: who art thou that judgest another?"*

What we need to kill is ourselves, not in suicide, but in death to self (our flesh). We need to die to our desire, lust, and envy and learn to give of ourselves and walk upright before the LORD. That is the point of this interaction, this cohabitation, as man could learn to love each other and give of ourselves to ensure others have a better life.

There is therefore now no condemnation to them which are in Christ Jesus, who walk not after the flesh, but after the Spirit (Romans 8:1). This scripture speaks to the liberty afforded those who walk after the Spirit and not after the flesh. In truth, life—walking in the Spirit—is liberating. We are often told that Christianity is full of restraints and most that follow or seek to be a disciple of CHRIST often fail or garner hypocritical positions on sin, as they secretly are as carnal as the world while condemning all others.

I will share a truth that most pastors will not share. The Bible explains that, for those who have died to self and live unto the LORD, all things are permissible, but not all things are prudent. Paul explains it this way regarding him and the faith:

> "*12 All things are lawful unto me, but all things are not expedient: all things are lawful for me, but I will not be brought under the power of any.*
>
> *13 Meats for the belly, and the belly for meats: but God shall destroy both it and them. Now the body is not for fornication, but for the Lord; and the Lord for the body.*
>
> *14 And God hath both raised up the Lord, and will also raise up us by his own power.*
>
> *15 Know ye not that your bodies are the members of Christ? shall I then take the members of Christ, and make them the members of an harlot? God forbid.*"
>
> (1 Corinthians 6: 12 – 15)

Although all things are permissible, that does not make them right before the LORD, and they are subject to GOD's Word on spiritual and fleshly consequences. What we have to understand is that we have to die to self and live unto the LORD. 'What does that mean?' you may ask. It means that lust and desire of the flesh, fornicating, over eating for pleasure, drinking excessively, and like behavior are actions that speak to your desire to serve **you**, which is lust. They are attempts to satisfy the flesh and the fleshly desires you have, after being programmed by the noise.

The noise has you seeking selfish gratifications, which can't be fulfilled. They always leave you sad, drunk, hurt, and most all, belittled from the state you should be in to have dominion. These things mock you and give occasion for the accuser to bear witness of how far away you are from what you were created to be. The way to overcome is to die to self and live for CHRIST. Even though you are forgiven of sin, you have authority over your flesh and you can choose to walk after the Spirit or after the flesh, as is shown in Romans 6:1 – 19:

> "*1 What shall we say then? Shall we continue in sin, that grace may abound?*
>
> *2 God forbid. How shall we, that are dead to sin, live any longer therein?*
>
> *3 Know ye not, that so many of us as were baptized into Jesus Christ were baptized into his death?*
>
> *4 Therefore we are buried with him by baptism into death: that like as Christ was raised up from the dead*

by the glory of the Father, even so we also should walk in newness of life.

5 *For if we have been planted together in the likeness of his death, we shall be also in the likeness of his resurrection:*

6 *Knowing this, that our old man is crucified with him, that the body of sin might be destroyed, that henceforth we should not serve sin.*

7 *For he that is dead is freed from sin.*

8 *Now if we be dead with Christ, we believe that we shall also live with him:*

9 *Knowing that Christ being raised from the dead dieth no more; death hath no more dominion over him.*

10 *For in that he died, he died unto sin once: but in that he liveth, he liveth unto God.*

11 *Likewise reckon ye also yourselves to be dead indeed unto sin, but alive unto God through Jesus Christ our Lord.*

12 *Let not sin therefore reign in your mortal body, that ye should obey it in the lusts thereof.*

13 *Neither yield ye your members as instruments of unrighteousness unto sin: but yield yourselves unto God, as those that are alive from the dead, and your members as instruments of righteousness unto God.*

14 *For sin shall not have dominion over you: for ye are not under the law, but under grace.*

15 *What then? shall we sin, because we are not under the law, but under grace? God forbid.*

16 *Know ye not, that to whom ye yield yourselves servants to obey, his servants ye are to whom ye obey; whether of sin unto death, or of obedience unto righteousness?*

17 *But God be thanked, that ye were the servants of sin, but ye have obeyed from the heart that form of doctrine which was delivered you.*

18 *Being then made free from sin, ye became the servants of righteousness.*

19 *I speak after the manner of men because of the infirmity of your flesh: for as ye have yielded your members servants to uncleanness and to iniquity unto iniquity; even so now yield your members servants to righteousness unto holiness."*

You have authority over your flesh, having had it subjected to death through baptism with CHRIST and more so into its resurrection. Now as the scripture says, live unto righteousness, after having survived death and resurrected through faith. That is why there is so much scripture in this writing because faith cometh by hearing and hearing from the Word of GOD.

We should not allow ourselves to be the very reason we live in misery, doubt, and despair. We should not allow ourselves to suffer slow agonizing deaths, living in fear and doubting our existence. We fail to enjoy what has been created for us. Turning to drugs, drinking, and sex for temporary fixes is never the solution. The answer to releasing disappointment is to live, love, and learn. Live unto GOD by loving each other and learn of Him (GOD), so you can understand what the plan is for your life. I assure you it is not enough to go to work for some company that pays you as little as they can to keep you on board, giving a tenth of that pay to a pastor who holds you hostage in guilt, and then retire, grow old, and wait on the early bird special. GOD forbid! Once you die to self, you will be able to live a life that leaves a legacy that bears witness to your love of GOD and your obedience and a dedication to serving others.

You can choose to have a life that sees creation but doesn't have its sight set on some all-inclusive retreat where you spend all the time eating and drinking and laying by the pool. Walk in the faith and meet folk from all over, and you will find that you share so much in common. Live a life that leaves a legacy that says you cared to leave an inheritance for your children's children and asserts you laid your hand to the task and gave your all. In order to do this, it takes commitment.

GOD is committed to the order He has established. He does not change the rules midstream. Since creation, GOD has been committed to ensuring we have right relationship with Him. He is GOD ALMIGHTY, and He changes not. Yet He has prepared for us, since creation, a way to have fellowship with Him and creation. That fellowship is dependent on our faith and our level of commitment.

Chapter 8

COMMITMENT

S uccess in a relationship, or I should say harmony, is based on the reality established when relationship is formed. When GOD created man, He did not create a man that would die, or be down-trodden, sad, enslaved, or abused. GOD created a man and gave him dominion (sovereignty or control) over all creation. Then He assigned a task to Adam.

> *"He was to tend to the garden which he presided over and lived within, And, then, Lord God took the man, and put him into the garden of Eden to dress it and to keep it" (Genesis 2:15). Then GOD endowed him with dominion, and fellowship with all creation, as GOD brought all creation before Adam, and whatsoever he named it, that's what it was."*
>
> (Genesis 2:19)

Then GOD fellowshipped with Adam and walked with him in the cool of the day, where He shared with Adam the order of creation and the effects of his interactions with creation. The knowledge GOD shared with Adam was Truth, as GOD is not a man that He can lie. This is how Adam knew that it was out of GOD's order for him to eat of the tree of the knowledge of good and evil. Within the order GOD created was a committed order that would not yield to self, lust or evil. There was no reset. There was a path that moved forward that required actions to offset the effects of disobedience, which is sin and warrants death.

GOD, in his gracious and merciful, committed relationship to man and order, provided a Savior to restore the relationship between He, man, creation, the commitment and order that He established in the beginning. All—everything—could have, and should have, perished at the rebellion of Adam against GOD and the order of creation. GOD's love for us has created a path for us to better understand the full balance He established with order. It allows us to enjoy creation and his fellowship through a committed relationship.

"*Go and sin no more*" JESUS bid folk to do this after healing them and absolving them of sin. This is to request that they be committed to the order of righteousness and fellowship with the Creator and creation. We must be committed to the order GOD has established as it will not yield or change. (Mercy and grace are not affirmations for repentance from GOD.) Mercy is GOD holding back judgment that is due us, often because of CHRIST and always because of love. Grace is the power of his love for us that is bestowed us even beyond our failures.

GOD is perfect in this that his order does not change and is what commitment is. We have to ask ourselves: what are we committed to? If we have not died to self and accepted CHRIST as Savior, we are often committed to dying and chasing a feeling that continuously evades us because it can't be fulfilled in the flesh. A committed relationship means that you have burned the ships that could take you back to your old ways, and you have accepted the order of engagement (the work needed) from the Word. Committed means you are faithful that your work and efforts will yield peace and joy, which are fruit of the Spirit, and not succumb to the noise of contrary opinions.

We often have relationships where we confess commitment, but our actions are to the contrary, so our results are to the contrary. You cannot tell me (well, you could, but you would be lying) that you are walking after the Spirit while you are fornicating, engaging in adultery, and drenched in sin. This is rebellion to GOD's order for the righteousness of GOD. It does not mean that you are not saved, or betrothed, to a covenant relationship; it means you are not committed to making it work.

Most marriages do not work because of lack of commitment, not money issues, but where your heart is committed is where your treasure will be. The money issue is a reflection of lack of commitment to each other because, where the money is, is where the commitment lies. The order is established for how creation works regarding how walking after the Spirit or the flesh yields results. The marriage bond is a covenant that will yield results based on an established order. If you are committed to holding each other up, keeping each other accountable, and in an established reality of the power of the Word of GOD being absolute truth, there is unity of purpose. The commitment to that order will yield the fruit of the Spirit. If there is rebellion to that order and no commitment or a loose (insincere) commitment, it will yield the fleshly results. This lack of commitment is why many folk are miserable, commit adultery, yell, fight, drink and cuss each other out. It is because they are uncommitted. It does not matter that he or she does not know that you are not committed. GOD knows and His order is established. You can't hide.

Adam and Eve tried to hide, but the sin was done and, as sin does. It seeks to expose you and mock you. Sin, when discovered, tries to blame others and to deny authority over the choices made, as Adam said *"And the man said, 'The woman whom thou gavest to be with me, she gave me of the tree, and I did eat' (Genesis 3:13),"* placing blame on GOD and Eve. One of the lessons of this response is that GOD did not just say, "Well, okay," and just send them on to die (which they did die that day, they did not cease). He, with the established order, shed the blood of an innocent lamb (as He did with us through JESUS CHRIST), and covered them from their sin. The wage is paid, but the order is not broken, so fellowship may remain.

You can't have idols in your life and be committed to something or someone else. You are the servant of the GOD you obey or the order you obey, which has its own set of consequences or results. Romans 6:16 tells us, *"16 Know ye not, that to whom ye yield yourselves servants to obey, his servants ye are to whom ye obey; whether of sin unto death, or of obedience unto righteousness?"* You don't have to be caught to be guilty. Idols today may not look like the idols of old, but they have the same ramifications. You don't have to have a giant golden bull or a statue you carry, but anything you exalt above the established order of GOD is an idol. The truth is, in most cases, idols are symbols of rebellion and selfishness. As I stated earlier, we create gods we can tote. We place our desires as their power, and then submit to ourselves through them. *We* are the evil, not the material. Gold is not evil. We are, as we worship our lusts through it. Money is not evil, as the Word says, *"For the love of money is the root of all evil: which while some coveted after, they have erred from the faith, and pierced themselves through with many sorrows" (Timothy 6:10).* There is no evil in material. There is no certain type of wood, metal, or water that is evil. Man impresses his desire upon a thing and makes that thing the confirmation of his wicked heart. Whether a man sacrifices his heart, time, or resources to a thing, it is not compelling. It is a <u>thing</u>. There are times when a logo (a man-made symbol) speaks to a culture and serves as indicator of an associated lifestyle, but in truth it is a symbol of the collective hearts of men that empower it, which takes commitment to selfishness and lusts.

GOD is clear that we are not to hold up graven images or create idols because He is our source—the only Creator. Looking to lottery winnings, wagering on chance, or submitting to others' principles for your sustenance is not commitment to GOD. Let me bring this home. If a woman is married to a man, yet she allows another man to take care of her, who has her loyalty? To who is she committed? She is committed to herself, yet one man facilitates her desire. Which man can make demands? The Word says in Matthew 6:21– 24:

*"21 For where your treasure is, there will your heart be
also.*

*22 The light of the body is the eye: if therefore thine eye
be single, thy whole body shall be full of light.*

*23 But if thine eye be evil, thy whole body shall be full
of darkness. If therefore the light that is in thee be
darkness, how great is that darkness!*

*24 No man can serve two masters: for either he will hate
the one, and love the other; or else he will hold to the
one, and despise the other. Ye cannot serve God and
mammon."*

You can't serve two masters with all your heart. Where your
heart is, that is where you will spend your money and your time.
People can tell you anything. The question is: Do they know the
Truth? Do they truly understand where their commitment lies?
Some folk will say they don't, and then they deny the HOLY
SPIRIT because it will convict you, and let you know. If you do
not have the HOLY SPIRIT, then you are not saved, and you
need to pray for deliverance. I know there is some contention
here, as some believe that, once you confess the LORD as Savior,
you are filled with the HOLY GHOST. Others believe that the
HOLY GHOST will fall on you when you are ready, and you
will bear evidence by speaking in tongues. The Truth is that
CHRIST promised a Comforter who knows all things and that
He would indwell us. This is the most powerful dispensation man
has known, not GOD leading us by pillar of fire and cloud, not

GOD directing us by prophet, but GOD indwelling us. That's commitment to your salvation.

How committed are you to your salvation? Living the lie in sin will continue to yield the wages of sin and renew the commitment to sin. Go before GOD and confess your sin, and be cleansed in the blood of CHRIST, whose sinless life and shed blood covers a multitude of sins. Go and sin no more. REPENT! Sure you will make mistakes, but your commitment to living a Christ-driven life will govern your actions because it will be dependent on your faith and belief. Mercy and grace preside within GOD's order. Know that you are his in the covenant, and He is committed to your growth. Paul writes to the Philippians that he is "*Being confident of this very thing, that he which hath begun a good work in you will perform it until the day of Jesus Christ (Philippians 1:6)."*

Most people are not solely committed to being evil or forsaking the LORD. They have moments where they are willing to rebel, even wrestle with issues or topics that spark anger and rebellion. I had a wise man tell me that "you can't be angry with someone unless you judge them first." There are people or races or religions, even whole countries of people, whereby folk will refuse to extend love or be gracious because they have judged them unworthy. *"A little leaven leaveneth the whole lump"* *(Galatians 5:9)*. It only takes a little evil and selfishness to begin a series of qualifiers or judgments for rebellion.

We start out by stating matters we will not yield to, like being yelled at or being mistreated, which turns into summoning anger and ill temperament (that we regard as having spunk or a backbone), lodged against folk in situations where we should extend grace. We do not trust GOD for deliverance, so we develop strongholds—places we keep from the LORD where we may retreat. In these areas, we believe that the order of GOD does not matter as they are our refuge. We retreat into pornography to handle stress and loneliness, alcohol to handle the same or to relieve stress, and we loosen our resolve to even sin more. Sex, drugs, lies, anger, wrath, other relationships (the wages of the flesh), or simply shutting down from the world. We establish places we do not allow the LORD to be sovereign. We do not allow Him into these places because we are not fully convinced in our hearts that He will love us enough to heal us there. We are not committed to the relationship and transparency. Even more direct, these are areas in our flesh that we have developed to handle the world that we have not turned over to GOD.

We have to understand and believe that GOD is a rock and a strong place. His Word and his Spirit reside in us and can handle any matter. *"The Lord is good, a strong hold in the day of trouble; and he knoweth them that trust in him (Nahum 1:7)."* We have to trust the LORD completely and be committed to the relationship of restoration that can only be manifested by surrendering to the LORD. Pride is a stronghold we build whereby we resolve the loss of dignity is unbearable.

We do not consider the loss of dignity CHRIST endured that He may die for us, so He could ensure so we could have fellowship with GOD ALMIGHTY. He wanted to ensure that we can be saved from condemnation and eternal darkness. You do not consider that the LORD of Lords and KING of

Kings became a curse and hung on a tree, forgoing all dignity and grace for us. You're upset because someone disrespected you, and you are unwilling to give grace and mercy to those folk, after receiving it from CHRIST by who you were redeemed. We have to be fully committed to LORD in trust and in faith to have breakthroughs that tear down the strongholds in our lives. I love the book of Job where GOD explains who He is in relationship to creation:

> "*1 Then the Lord answered Job out of the whirlwind, and said,*
>
> *2 Who is this that darkeneth counsel by words without knowledge?*
>
> *3 Gird up now thy loins like a man; for I will demand of thee, and answer thou me.*
>
> *4 Where wast thou when I laid the foundations of the earth? declare, if thou hast understanding.*
>
> *5 Who hath laid the measures thereof, if thou knowest? or who hath stretched the line upon it?*
>
> *6 Whereupon are the foundations thereof fastened? or who laid the corner stone thereof;*
>
> *7 When the morning stars sang together, and all the sons of God shouted for joy?*
>
> *8 Or who shut up the sea with doors, when it brake forth, as if it had issued out of the womb?*
>
> *9 When I made the cloud the garment thereof, and thick darkness a swaddling band for it,*

¹⁰ *And brake up for it my decreed place, and set bars and doors,*

¹¹ *And said, Hitherto shalt thou come, but no further: and here shall thy proud waves be stayed?*

¹² *Hast thou commanded the morning since thy days; and caused the dayspring to know his place;*

¹³ *That it might take hold of the ends of the earth, that the wicked might be shaken out of it?*

¹⁴ *It is turned as clay to the seal; and they stand as a garment.*

¹⁵ *And from the wicked their light is withholden, and the high arm shall be broken.*

¹⁶ *Hast thou entered into the springs of the sea? or hast thou walked in the search of the depth?*

¹⁷ *Have the gates of death been opened unto thee? or hast thou seen the doors of the shadow of death?*

¹⁸ *Hast thou perceived the breadth of the earth? declare if thou knowest it all.*

¹⁹ *Where is the way where light dwelleth? and as for darkness, where is the place thereof,*

²⁰ *That thou shouldest take it to the bound thereof, and that thou shouldest know the paths to the house thereof?*

²¹ *Knowest thou it, because thou wast then born? or because the number of thy days is great?*

²² *Hast thou entered into the treasures of the snow? or hast thou seen the treasures of the hail,*

23 *Which I have reserved against the time of trouble, against the day of battle and war?*

24 *By what way is the light parted, which scattereth the east wind upon the earth?*

25 *Who hath divided a watercourse for the overflowing of waters, or a way for the lightning of thunder;*

26 *To cause it to rain on the earth, where no man is; on the wilderness, wherein there is no man;*

27 *To satisfy the desolate and waste ground; and to cause the bud of the tender herb to spring forth?*

28 *Hath the rain a father? or who hath begotten the drops of dew?*

29 *Out of whose womb came the ice? and the hoary frost of heaven, who hath gendered it?*

30 *The waters are hid as with a stone, and the face of the deep is frozen.*

31 *Canst thou bind the sweet influences of Pleiades, or loose the bands of Orion?*

32 *Canst thou bring forth Mazzaroth in his season? or canst thou guide Arcturus with his sons?*

33 *Knowest thou the ordinances of heaven? canst thou set the dominion thereof in the earth?*

34 *Canst thou lift up thy voice to the clouds, that abundance of waters may cover thee?*

35 *Canst thou send lightnings, that they may go and say unto thee, Here we are?*

36 *Who hath put wisdom in the inward parts? or who hath given understanding to the heart?*

37 *Who can number the clouds in wisdom? or who can stay the bottles of heaven,*

38 *When the dust groweth into hardness, and the clods cleave fast together?*

39 *Wilt thou hunt the prey for the lion? or fill the appetite of the young lions,*

40 *When they couch in their dens, and abide in the covert to lie in wait?*

41 *Who provideth for the raven his food? when his young ones cry unto God, they wander for lack of meat."*

This scripture shows the power of GOD over all things, from the majesty of creation to the order of clouds and elementals to the desire of animals to feed. Nothing is too great or too small for GOD because He is the GOD of creation. Folk will not allow GOD into the dark places of their hearts because they don't trust and believe in GOD. You trust what you rely on. We have to be trained out of that. We have to determine this whole thing is real, not just an amalgamation of stories, fairy tales and people full of game. What I hope to show is that you can commit your life to the order GOD has established in his Word—not to what your pastor or preacher says (although he or she should be confirming what you read and the experiences you are having). We must trust that his order will yield what He said it would.

I had a friend tell me that he confessed and gave testimony to people so much concerning the works of what GOD had done in his life that GOD had to uphold them because folk would believe GOD had not done his job. I laugh at the story because he proclaimed healing years ago from a threatening issue and a seriously potentially progressive issue and never went back to the doctor regarding the issue, accepting his healing. He finally went back to the doctor and had his faith confirmed. He says he hangs his hat on that issue in his life to confirm GOD is real.

Have you had a "GOD is real" moment? GOD is faithful to take the issues of life and confirm his reality to you. Now I have another friend who confesses he has given GOD many opportunities to be real to him with many projects and lottery chances, and GOD has not shown up once. I assert GOD has shown up every time because, if he had the money, he would be a problem. Until his heart changes, he is better off broke. GOD is not a genie that He should serve you, or a prostitute that He should serve you for your gain. GOD is almighty and sovereign and, when we realize He is the ALMIGHTY GOD authority— sovereign ruler of all things—we can find out what it is He has for us to do and how we should live and commit to it.

As I stated earlier, my life has been full of situations where I was at my wits end. On some occasions, it should have been my life's end, but I survived. This is simply because there is no situation too great for GOD. He protects and keeps us because we are His. This does not speak to some power I have, but solely of the power and might of GOD. The issue is, not so much as surrendering, but one of crying out. There is a song by the musical group Take 6 that I used to play over and over, where they say "He can make a way out of no way exchange lonely nights for brighter days," and it was my mantra in hard times, along with Psalms 31 and 71. I was challenging the Lord, not with indignation, but with a sorrowful hopeful plea, that He would be with me as He was with David. He has never failed me because He is real to me, and He loves me. I pray His grace and mercy will abide with me forever, and I pray that you would know Him as your Lord and Savior and that He will be real to you.

I know we trust what works, but we can't decide what "working" looks like either. GOD knows what is best for you, and sometimes His answer does not look like what you decided is best for you. The issue is a matter of Truth. What is your truth? I often say that, when you know the Truth, it replaces what you believed to be truth. Those sailors, sailing towards the horizon with expectations of falling eventually, never did, and they came back to where they started from—in the other direction. They knew the world was not flat as they once believed. The truth is that the world is round, and they had to discover the truth before it became truth to them.

How many fallacies do you believe? How many wives' tales, superstitions, lies, and folk tales have you accepted as truth that have nothing to do with what is really true? Sure, it is your reality, and you operate in it as truth, with results that are manageable or never conflicting with truth, so they remain real to you, even though they are not truths. Truth is the order GOD has established for creation, and it is absolute. It may not be realized by you, as you may not have heard it or interpreted it. Maybe it has not rubbed up against your fallacy, but there is absolute Truth. In order for you to commit to GOD and his order, you must accept his Word as Truth, or you will continue to use what makes you comfortable the reality you can tolerate. This reality, in most cases, is a lie and not the truth. Call it a gray area, but it is a black lie.

Chapter 9

TRUTH

have heard the argument that the Bible is not the truth of GOD. I have heard that Shakespeare wrote the King James Version of the Bible so he could have a homosexual relationship with the King of England. There is one saying that says it was written to control slaves. Others state that it is missing books, and it is an incomplete work. I have heard scholars say it is not literal and is filled with metaphors that are open to interpretation. There are enough doubters and naysayers that there are books on why the Bible is not truth. When you have sailed the world, you can speak of what you have seen on the voyage. When you have not, you can only speculate. I have seen GOD work in my life and in the lives of others. I have relied on the Word of GOD (the Bible) to help establish Truth in my life.

I gave this a lot of thought and considered critical thinking models to separate fallacy from Truth in an attempt to convince folk that the Bible speaks Truth. I considered stating an argument and then utilizing critical thinking analytics to resolve the matter, but I subscribe to the thought process more intently which states:

"That which will demonstrate a truth to one person, possibly will never move another. Because our reason does not consist in a mathematical point: and the heart of reason, that vital and most sensible part, in which only it can be conquered fairly, is an ambulatory essence, and not fixed: it wanders up and down like a floating island, or like that which we call the life blood."   (Taylor, 1660)

No matter how well I convey a point, there will be naysayers. The arguments will shift, and all types of issues come into play that is not even germane to whether the Word is GOD's Truth or not. Folk dispute the Bible as Truth, and that it was written on the hearts of men by GOD. What can I say that will convince a man?...The Truth has to be spoken into a man's heart which must be ready to receive it.

Truth is not universal. It does not appeal to everyone no matter where they are in their life. Some folk will be offended by the Truth because the path they are on is so far from aligning with it. They are offended as they see it as a judgment against their character and intellect to be that far off. The Truth is beneficial for all, universally, because it is established by the Creator as a guide for *all* men. The Gospels of Matthew, Mark, and Luke give an illustration of seed falling on soil as a story about Truth falling on men's hearts and where they are in life can determine how it is received. (I will use Matthew 18:3 – 9.):

"³ And he spake many things unto them in parables, saying, Behold, a sower went forth to sow;

⁴ And when he sowed, some seeds fell by the way side, and the fowls came and devoured them up.

⁵ Some fell upon stony places, where they had not much earth: and forthwith they sprung up, because they had no deepness of earth:

⁶ And when the sun was up, they were scorched; and because they had no root, they withered away.

⁷ And some fell among thorns; and the thorns sprung up, and choked them.

⁸ But other fell into good ground, and brought forth fruit, some an hundredfold, some sixtyfold, some thirtyfold.

⁹ Who hath ears to hear, let him hear."

Seed is seed. It is a constant in the parable, like the Truth, which it symbolizes. The wayside seed, as CHRIST explains later, fell on those who have no relationship with CHRIST and those distracted by the noise from the enemy that was heard above the Word. Folk came and deterred the folk who should receive it. Then, there is the man who receives the Word, but has no place of growth and encouragement. The order of GOD is strange to him. When he received the Word, it resonated well. It bodes well in his heart but, when it is challenged, he has no support. So when hardships came, or he endures a trial, he is offended. And, then, there is he who receives the Word among naysayers and unbelievers—those who are hard-hearted and decidedly rebellious. Finally, there is the man who hears the Word, believes it, and is ready for it, so much so that he shares it and others believe.

Simply, because you do not believe in a thing, does not make it a lie. There are those who know the Truth and do not abide in it. They later have a change of actions predicated on the Truth being there. I like discussing Solomon because he was wise. He spoke with GOD or heard from GOD and, yet, he still served other gods even when he knew it was wrong. The truth is if you serve yourself only, the Truth will fail you. It's not why we are here. If you serve GOD, there is growth and abundance. Solomon speaks in Ecclesiastes of having seen sunrises and sunsets, eating and drinking, possessions and interactions with folk on all levels—from loving to dying, wealth and poverty, ownership and freedom, being old and young—and concludes that, if it does not serve GOD and follow His order, it is all vanity.

Selfishness separates us from Truth often, as we decide that we will have the Truth serve us instead of us serving the Truth. Once you hear Truth, you will immediately know how close you are to it. If you are deeply offended and find that this is completely contrary to what you believe, in most cases, you will judge the Truth as a lie. If you find the Truth is in line with where you are in life, you will probably accept it easier. Truth tells us where we are because it is a standard like the North Star or magnetic North.

Truth is not in different places for many people to find on many different walks. The Truth bears witness to CHRIST. CHRIST fulfills the Word of GOD as GOD became flesh and walked among us and sent his HOLY SPIRIT to indwell us that knows Truth. The Word is Truth, which is CHRIST and CHRIST who is JESUS. JESUS exclaimed, "...*I am the way, the truth, and the life: no man cometh unto the Father, but by me*" *(John 14:16)*. There is one Truth–one way to GOD and right fellowship. It is through CHRIST JESUS. This is the Truth.

The point of Truth is not to bring torment to men, but to show the way to, and of, GOD. Truth is to torment evil and expose it as evil so it can flee from man, and man can move from it. CHRIST came upon men who had evil spirits, blocking the way so no man could pass. (This is what evil noise does, blocking the way for man.) JESUS's very presence as Truth (as He is the Truth, the way, and the life) tormented evil (as fear does), and evil sought to flee. Take note of Matthew 8:28:

> "*28 And when he was come to the other side into the country of the Gergesenes, there met him two possessed with devils, coming out of the tombs, exceeding fierce, so that no man might pass by that way.*
>
> *29 And, behold, they cried out, saying, What have we to do with thee, Jesus, thou Son of God? art thou come hither to torment us before the time?*
>
> *30 And there was a good way off from them an herd of many swine feeding.*
>
> *31 So the devils besought him, saying, If thou cast us out, suffer us to go away into the herd of swine.*
>
> *32 And he said unto them, Go. And when they were come out, they went into the herd of swine: and, behold, the*

*whole herd of swine ran violently down a steep place
into the sea, and perished in the waters."*

The men are free from their torment, wet evil is tormented and encapsulated in drowning pigs, and the way is made clear for other men because of the Truth. If you will read this scripture, you will notice that there are those who are having a degree of consternation at the loss of revenue—at the cost of freedom—brought about by Truth, as their pigs are dead. It is the case often that there are those who will seek to benefit from the effects of evil and the hold it has on men. There are news outlets and many other amplifiers of noise that benefit on the stagnant nature of man because he listens to the noise and is arrested in his development by it. Without Truth, there is no growth, as the way is blocked and a man is held captive.

Why do doctors want us all on some kind of medication that alters our reality and our ability to process and cope with Truth? It is so they can profit and be the only ones <u>not</u> on meds. I had a doctor ask me: "How is it that you are not on any meds?" And I asked him, what meds was he on?…(Nothing.) Not that you can't be on meds or shouldn't take meds, but there are folk who are on everything from stress to sleep medicine, curbing your body's natural order to be uncomfortable with noise and seek truth. Medicated folk are more compliant and less involved, yet just as aware because the matter is spiritual.

John the Baptist came speaking Truth as a herald to the living Word. He is described as a man in the desert, eating locusts for meat and wild honey. He spoke Truth to Herod. And, JESUS and righteous men came and were baptized as they heard Truth. Those who were far from the Truth were offended as John called out the religious leaders of the time for being ineffective and ungodly—Matthew 3:4 – 12:

> "*4 And the same John had his raiment of camel's hair, and a leathern girdle about his loins; and his meat was locusts and wild honey.*
>
> *5 Then went out to him Jerusalem, and all Judaea, and all the region round about Jordan,*
>
> *6 And were baptized of him in Jordan, confessing their sins.*
>
> *7 But when he saw many of the Pharisees and Sadducees come to his baptism, he said unto them, O generation of vipers, who hath warned you to flee from the wrath to come?*
>
> *8 Bring forth therefore fruits meet for repentance:*
>
> *9 And think not to say within yourselves, We have Abraham to our father: for I say unto you, that God is able of these stones to raise up children unto Abraham.*
>
> *10 And now also the axe is laid unto the root of the trees: therefore every tree which bringeth not forth good fruit is hewn down, and cast into the fire.*
>
> *11 I indeed baptize you with water unto repentance. but he that cometh after me is mightier than I, whose shoes I am not worthy to bear: he shall baptize you with the Holy Ghost, and with fire:*

> *12 Whose fan is in his hand, and he will thoroughly*
> *purge his floor, and gather his wheat into the garner;*
> *but he will burn up the chaff with unquenchable fire."*

John the Baptist continued in this vein all the way to his death. He spoke Truth to Herod, and his brother Philip's wife (whom Herod had known) was cut to the core because she was living far from the Truth. So she desired to kill John—to silence him, but the Truth shouts in her heart and mind. Mark 6:18 – 20:

> *"18 For John had said unto Herod, "it is not lawful for*
> *thee to have thy brother's wife".*
> *19 Therefore, Herodias had a quarrel against him, and*
> *would have killed him; but she could not:*
> *20 For Herod feared John, knowing that he was a just*
> *man and an holy, and observed him; and when*
> *he heard him, he did many things, and heard him*
> *gladly."*

We often see in the Bible folk who brought the Truth killed by those who do not want to hear the Truth or be exposed by it. Stephen is stoned to death after he shares the Gospel, the good news, with people who chose to kill him rather than repent. The evil are tormented by the Truth Stephen relays, while CHRIST stands at the throne showing love and acceptance for the Truth that is spoken.

CHRIST JESUS came as the ransom for sin, the sacrifice for sin, and the atonement for sin, so man could continue on the path and accept Truth. You don't get to define Truth because you will make it suit you. The fact that sinners are offended by the Truth proves it is Truth. Truth has power because it is from GOD. Truth is the order GOD has established for how all creation interacts. GOD created harmony between man and all creation, as GOD granted man dominion over his creation. Man sinned by listening to noise—lies from the enemy—and established discord between him and creation since he took action contrary to the Truth GOD had established.

Even though man sinned, the order was established before creation for JESUS to be the solution to sin for man as GOD's truth made flesh and walking in the perfect order and authority of GOD's creation without sin (actions out of GOD's order). JESUS hereby cleared the path for man to have power over sin and to walk in restored order. That is the Gospel Truth, which takes faith to accept as reality. Faith is the substance of things hoped for the evidence of things unseen. Without faith, it is impossible to please GOD because faith comes by the Truth, which is the Word of GOD. By hearing the Word of GOD, we have faith established. Yet faith without works is nothing.

We must walk in what we believe because we are the servants of the GOD we obey. But, through the HOLY SPIRIT, we have the power, the authority, and the knowledge to walk upright in perfect order and serve the Truth. We must walk after the Spirit (which guides us) and not after the flesh (willful, selfish desire, which can't be satisfied and seeks to kill you). In walking after the Spirit, we bear fruit of the Spirit in our lives which is love, joy, peace, forbearance, kindness, goodness, faithfulness, gentleness and self-control. Against such things there is no law because this is proof that a man is in harmony and order with GOD, to which there need be no interference from law. In this order, there is proof that the man is walking in the order of GOD and no longer malfunctioning. When a man is no longer malfunctioning, it opens the door for harmonious interaction with GOD's creation and bears the fruit of the Spirit.

I talk to men often who struggle with selfishness because they are constantly pursuing the brass ring (status, wealth, power). This is lust. The Word says there are only three things: the lust of the eye, the lust of the flesh, and the pride of life. Sometimes it is important to have others around who hold you accountable and confirm that you are, or are not, delusional. This is why it is important to have a body of believers with whom you share your journey about your committed relationship with GOD. This collection of believers should comprise of members of the Church who share in our desire to learn more Truth.

Chapter 10

THE CHURCH

When we think of the church, many images come to mind. We think of a the old building with three doors so the FATHER, the SON, and the HOLY GHOST can enter, a small vestibule and one big room with wooden pews. Often there is a baptismal under the pulpit, or behind the choir stand. Sometimes there are 12 stain glass windows with pictures of each of the 12 apostles, each window dedicated by an organization or board member. The pews are filled on the back side with hymnals and funeral home fans with pictures of Martin Luther King or White JESUS. Between the hymnals holders are the little holders for communion juice cup holders and ink pens. This was the church of my youth.

Now, churches have these grand halls with lights and sound systems. Huge monitors are all around so there is not a bad seat, and overflow rooms with HD TV are usually housed below, so no one can miss the JESUS show and every dollar can be collected. Engaged weekly in bombastic praise and worship services, I have seen churches with bookstores, coffee shops and heard of some with ATM machines and VIP valet parking.

In truth, it does not matter what the building looks like, *none* of these pastors have been ordained by GOD to rebuild the temple in Israel or duplicate it anywhere else. These edifices are meant to impress the parishioners, not to rise to GOD's standards. The building means very little. When the Word of GOD speaks of the Church, it is speaking of the collective body of believers, the Ecclesia (body of believers).

The Bible first mentions the word "church" in Matthew 16:18 as CHRIST addresses Peter and tells him that he (Peter) is the rock on which He will build His Church. There was no church prior to this as there was no body of believers. Christ had not come, had not died for the sins of the world, nor had He been resurrected. There was nothing to believe in prior to CHRIST because there was a different dispensation, or process, for godly relationships or fellowship.

To be saved one must believe JESUS is the Son of GOD, who walked the earth without sin, was crucified, died for all the sins of the world, and was raised from the dead. That is the faith of believers, the basis of the Church, and the body of believers— the Truth. Any other groups of people who believe in a different path to salvation are a group of people who believe in a different path of salvation. They are <u>not</u> the church. Most Christians do not even know what salvation is.

I remember when I first said the sinner's prayer and heard Christians refer to people as saved, they were referring to the manner in which believers *behaved or carried their salvation.* They spoke of pious (deeply religious reverence of GOD) folk, who seemed to be happy most times. They did not drink, smoke, curse, or fornicate. Sometimes they were mean folk who held harsh judgments for everyone else and were judgmental about anything that seemed like fun. Whatever the understanding of who was actually saved, the examples seemed to be people who had given up on life, remained close to the church (the building), and were content with listening to gospel music, watching Jubilee, and The 700 Hundred Club. (GOD forbid.) There is nothing wrong with those folk. I just can't see youth and vibrancy, filled with personality and zeal, when we are confined to this existence only. It is not the example given by saved folk in the Bible. Let's tackle this by first understanding salvation. What is salvation, who is saved, and what are we being saved from?

I love the Old Testament because we see the direct interaction with GOD, man, and the prophets speaking to GOD and hearing from GOD explaining the Word of GOD so man could live. (I have had preachers say the heart of GOD speaks of his intent for man.) I believe salvation prayed for in the Old Testament referred to salvation from the wrath of GOD for evil. When you read the Old Testament, it speaks of action needed for salvation. In the book of Numbers, there are cries to be saved from the enemies of Israel, and in Psalm there are cries to be saved from drought, enemies and atrocities. In Isaiah and Jeremiah there is a different perspective that speaks to a person being saved—truly saved and there being a peace about him because the strength of the LORD is with them. The prophet Isaiah speaks to eternal salvation as it is written in Isaiah 45:16-18:

"16 They shall be ashamed, and also confounded, all of them: they shall go to confusion together that are makers of idols.

17 But Israel shall be saved in the Lord with an everlasting salvation: ye shall not be ashamed nor confounded world without end.

18 For thus saith the Lord that created the heavens; God himself that formed the earth and made it; he hath established it, he created it not in vain, he formed it to be inhabited: I am the Lord; and there is none else."

This is powerful to me because it references CHRIST in the Old Testament, and it speaks to exclusivity of salvation as it says, "I am the Lord and there is none else." The Lord JESUS CHRIST is the only way to salvation, and it speaks to the order GOD established and that He made the world to be lived upon, to be inhabited. GOD did not create the world for there to be constant conflict between its inhabitants. He created the world to be full of peace and love. Man has chosen to be greedy, possessive, and filled with lusts that he seeks to fulfill.

Here we also understand that those who are not ashamed of the LORD shall be saved. Openly denying the ways of the flesh and walking after the Spirit opens up the world to Truth as GOD intended a man to live upon it, without fear of anything on it. That is the first salvation. The second salvation that is afforded believers is the salvation from the wrath of GOD at judgment. I am not saying that GOD has changed salvation. It is clear that we should fear the GOD of our body and soul, knowing He has always been our salvation. I am saying that, in the Old Testament, we see more prayers for salvation from physical threats, while later in the New Testament it is apparent that our immortal souls are subject to the judgment and wrath of GOD.

Salvation is to be saved from the repercussions of sin. Those folk who have accepted CHRIST as the intermediary between GOD's wrath and GOD's love have realized that there is nothing that they could do to overcome sin but to accept CHRIST's life as sacrifice for sin. It is perfect and eternal. Again, back in the days of sacrificial animals, men took animals to the altar before the priest (as specified for that sin) and said 'this is me,' and the priest killed the animal, blood was shed, and sin forgiven. This salvation was so that the wrath of GOD would not cause death, captivity, famine, or drought. It was flesh for fleshly actions. CHRIST JESUS having lived a life without sin, being both High Priest and Sacrificial Lamb (or all flesh for all sins), was sacrificed and death could not hold Him, as He is risen from the dead. The veil in the temple is rent (symbolizing that the barrier between GOD and man is gone) because CHRIST is now the way, the life, and the truth for all men who accept His sacrifice. The Church, the body of believers, are those who have accepted this sacrifice as themselves (their persons as the sacrificed flesh before the priests) and are seen before GOD through this act and are disciples to this life.

Being a "Disciple of CHRIST" can sound very serious, and it is, but what does it mean? It means the principles of the life of CHRIST as taught during CHRIST's time on earth are the doctrines and principles we live our lives by. How do we know what those are? We know them by reading His Word, coming together as a collective studying His Word, and practicing those principles together.

On the day of Pentecost those men ate together, shared the Word, praised GOD, and gave to one another as there was need. That is the way of the Church! We, as the Church, should be holding each other up, and there should be accountability, not judgment. What does that look like? It looks like the life of CHRIST. Mercifully, JESUS finds a lady caught in the act of adultery. He has her released from her accusers and bids her go and sin no more. He loved her through the fault. She was probably terrified. She understood that she was caught dead to rights and expected the penalty that she knew went along with the act. But, she was set free from death. I doubt if she would have allowed herself to be in that predicament again.

Then, there are the money changers in the temples and those that sold doves, who had no kindred to the order of sanctity of the process of sin forgiveness. That is to say, instead of them handling folk with contrite hearts seeking to get right with GOD through sacrifice, they sought gain and to make the burden harder than it is under the guise of being righteous folk. They were flogged and run off, as they violated the path to sin freedom just like the twins who were demon possessed. The evil had to be run off.

JESUS is love and mercy, but He was vigilant in calling out sin in folk. CHRIST did not cuss out disciples who were responding to the influence of the enemy. He rebuked the enemy, not the person. CHRIST was the Word, and He understood that *"we wrestle not against flesh and blood, but against principalities, against powers, against the rulers of the darkness of this world, against spiritual wickedness in high places" (Ephesians 6:12)*. He understands that people are precious and redeemable, as the question is asked, *"How can one say I love God, and hateth his brother, he is a liar: for he that loveth not his brother whom he hath seen, how can he love God whom he hath not seen?" (1 John 4:20)*.

The function of the Church is to love your neighbor and give of yourselves to ensure your neighbor's life. That looks like prayer, fellowship, and giving. If that is not being done, then, the collective you have is not a church. The greatest growth I've seen in my life was in a small group where we met, prayed, had accountability partners, and cared for one another. The enemy caused judgment on some folk against the affliction of other folk when we all were afflicted by sin. I know it sounds silly. How we can be in fellowship in the name of the LORD while accusing each other in the manner of the enemy? Paul and Peter did it to each other, so it will happen, but we have to be vigilant in our hearts not to entertain this mess.

Most church groups that I have seen in disarray are the product of gossip and judgmental believers. I love the way Paul would go into a church and just call out the sin and explain what the Word had to say about the action. He didn't call out the sinner. He addressed the sin. The Bible is clear about handling the matter. It states, if a brother be caught in a fault, those who are walking after the Spirit are to restore him in meekness, that is with tender mercy and love, seeking to be meek in the matter, and not with authority, power and judgment because, as the scripture goes on to say, "*you* might be tempted." There are at least several ways one who approaches someone caught in a fault might also be tripped up:

- Pride, thinking that you could not be caught up in something so silly yourself (You may be tested in that area.)
- Not having mercy and grace that has been extended you through CHRIST when your heart was contrite or broken
- Fear of losing a brother as he is shamed and feels unworthy to continue in the fellowship, there by losing a seed

Remember the parable of the seed. That the seed fell on good ground, but the ground was shallow. When the weeds sprang up to choke it out, there were no saints about to protect it. You are the saints that protect the seed. The saints plant, water, and tend, and GOD provides the increase. We are to tend the garden as it was appointed to Adam. We now know we are both the seed and the gardener. We have to tend to each other, and GOD will cause growth in our church. It is not the pastor's or preacher's job alone to tend to the body of believers. Paul did not live in Corinth, Ephesus, or Philippi, but the Word did live in the hearts of the Church and those committed to the discipleship of CHRIST.

We have to surrender our lives to GOD in intimacy to see how He chooses to use us as individuals before we will be much good to the collective. The surrender of self can be difficult because folk believe they are proud individuals meant to stand alone. JESUS had twelve disciples walk with Him, while being accountable for the world. Moses had Aaron and Joshua with him, while being accountable to all of Israel. David had mighty men of valor with him. I could go on about how the men of GOD had folk around them supporting the Word of GOD, challenging each other, and growing. In some cases, there was bickering, judgment, and power struggles, but the ones who surrendered to GOD, had an intimate relationship, and committed themselves to following GOD.

To have an individual relationship with GOD is to have the knowledge of who you are in relationship to creation, so that bickering and relationship-association mess does not deter you from what GOD has said. When we are committed to seeking intimacy, we understand the GOD of creation has established the order of life, and there is no other way by which a man can live peaceably on creation other than to surrender to the Creator and his order. How does one have an intimate relationship with GOD? GOD already knows everything about you, and his ways are higher than yours. So, how can you be intimate?

Chapter 11

INTIMACY

I feel a little giddy at the thought of intimacy, as it is a mature, serious thing. It is almost impossible to have an intimate relationship of value without knowing yourself and the person with which you are intimate. I equated intimacy to sex when I was younger and felt weird when my brother would speak with me about having intimacy with CHRIST and being the bride. In truth, intimacy is releasing your guard and allowing yourself to be known or familiar with someone. There is exclusivity because intimacy is privileged. Sure, there are levels of intimacy. I have been to concerts that boasted a close intimate performance, which meant you are close to the stage or artist. Seeing as though often there is not enough capacity for everyone to be "close," those who are "close" are privileged. Intimacy means there is potential for harm, based on proximity, and very few people will allow other people to get that close to them because there is little to no defense where there is intimacy. That is why it is important to choose well those with whom you are intimate, as intimacy produces vulnerability.

The vulnerability we have with GOD is always there. He is all powerful but, in the relationship with GOD, He offers his Son to live in us and for us to Trust in Him. GOD knows his Son completely and will know us through His sacrifice. I am reminded how the Israelites decided they wanted a King to go before them like the people whose land had been given to them. They had a way of order that did not demand sacrifice of them from insatiable flesh, but from Spirit which only required sacrifice to strengthen them and to ensure their growth. They chose a symbol of power instead of the ALMIGHTY POWER:

> "5 *And said unto him, Behold, thou art old, and thy sons walk not in thy ways: now make us a king to judge us like all the nations.*
>
> 6 *But the thing displeased Samuel, when they said, Give us a king to judge us. And Samuel prayed unto the Lord.*
>
> 7 *And the Lord said unto Samuel, Hearken unto the voice of the people in all that they say unto thee: for they have not rejected thee, but they have rejected me, that I should not reign over them.*
>
> 8 *According to all the works which they have done since the day that I brought them up out of Egypt even unto this day, wherewith they have forsaken me, and served other gods, so do they also unto thee.*

⁹ *Now therefore hearken unto their voice: howbeit*
yet protest solemnly unto them, and shew them the
manner of the king that shall reign over them."
(I Samuel 8: 5 – 9, KJV)

It reminds me of the young person who has been raised under the care and instruction of a loving father. This father has worked to ensure the child can cook for themselves and drive a vehicle. He has provided for them the clothes and the things that entertained and educated them. This father has helped with homework and driven that young person to all types of events and activities because he loves the child and wants them to be responsible and driven. Eventually, the child grows up. The father has saved up so the child can attend any college of their choice, and the child moves into the dorm room. The young adult seems to have forgotten every lesson learned and wants to go to the clubs and hang out. The young adult wants to be with people who have not been raised with a caring father. Those other people just want to party and have fun because they are not equipped and want to drag that young person down. They don't have skills and insights that the child has been given.

The children of Israel were being led by GOD ALMIGHTY and judged by his prophets who feared GOD and only sought to ensure there was right relations between GOD and the Israelites. Israel wanted to go to the "club" and hang out with folk who had rejected GOD so long ago they didn't even remember Him before the pagan gods they served. These gods could not even protect them from the Israelites subduing the land from them.

The Israelites wanted a king like those other folk. I often see a man who goes to work and breaks his back or racks his mind to eke out a living greater than what he had growing up only to find a wife who does not appreciate it. She wants to go to the club and hang out with single, unhappy women, who would secretly kill to be in her situation.

GOD in his ultimate display of free will—his love for us—allows them to have a king and understands there is no commitment or intimacy for Him from Israel. GOD does not abandon Israel, but He allows rebellion to have its course, as GOD's order does not change, but friction against it will either wear you down to disintegration or change your course. Where you end up is dependent upon how hard-hearted and stiff-necked you are.

GOD is committed to our salvation and allows us to get to know Him and see that He is kind, and faithful. We grow to the point where we can appreciate stability, knowledge, and faithfulness, and we can grow closer to the LORD as we begin to see the power of the Word and understand how GOD's order is better than the world. The world is seeking to kill us in the pursuit of flesh. We see that others are seeking to satiate the lust of the eye, the lust of the flesh, and the pride of life, and they are competing to see who can make who the most envious. Ephesians 4 speaks of the transformation that should take place in our lives as we move from carnal folk to carnal Christians to saints seeking after the Lord. We will evolve into people walking in the Spirit and not in the flesh, as we are prepared to be the Church, the bride of CHRIST washed and made ready:

"¹ I therefore, the prisoner of the Lord, beseech you that ye walk worthy of the vocation wherewith ye are called,

² With all lowliness and meekness, with longsuffering, forbearing one another in love;

³ Endeavouring to keep the unity of the Spirit in the bond of peace.

⁴ There is one body, and one Spirit, even as ye are called in one hope of your calling;

⁵ One Lord, one faith, one baptism,

⁶ One God and Father of all, who is above all, and through all, and in you all.

⁷ But unto every one of us is given grace according to the measure of the gift of Christ.

⁸ Wherefore he saith, When he ascended up on high, he led captivity captive, and gave gifts unto men.

⁹ (Now that he ascended, what is it but that he also descended first into the lower parts of the earth?

¹⁰ He that descended is the same also that ascended up far above all heavens, that he might fill all things.)

¹¹ And he gave some, apostles; and some, prophets; and some, evangelists; and some, pastors and teachers;

¹² For the perfecting of the saints, for the work of the ministry, for the edifying of the body of Christ:

¹³ Till we all come in the unity of the faith, and of the knowledge of the Son of God, unto a perfect man, unto the measure of the stature of the fulness of Christ:

¹⁴ *That we henceforth be no more children, tossed to and fro, and carried about with every wind of doctrine, by the sleight of men, and cunning craftiness, whereby they lie in wait to deceive;*

¹⁵ *But speaking the truth in love, may grow up into him in all things, which is the head, even Christ:*

¹⁶ *From whom the whole body fitly joined together and compacted by that which every joint supplieth, according to the effectual working in the measure of every part, maketh increase of the body unto the edifying of itself in love.*

¹⁷ *This I say therefore, and testify in the Lord, that ye henceforth walk not as other Gentiles walk, in the vanity of their mind,*

¹⁸ *Having the understanding darkened, being alienated from the life of God through the ignorance that is in them, because of the blindness of their heart:*

¹⁹ *Who being past feeling have given themselves over unto lasciviousness, to work all uncleanness with greediness.*

²⁰ *But ye have not so learned Christ;*

²¹ *If so be that ye have heard him, and have been taught by him, as the truth is in Jesus:*

²² *That ye put off concerning the former conversation the old man, which is corrupt according to the deceitful lusts;*

²³ *And be renewed in the spirit of your mind;*

²⁴ And that ye put on the new man, which after God is created in righteousness and true holiness.

²⁵ Wherefore putting away lying, speak every man truth with his neighbour: for we are members one of another.

²⁶ Be ye angry, and sin not: let not the sun go down upon your wrath:

²⁷ Neither give place to the devil.

²⁸ Let him that stole steal no more: but rather let him labour, working with his hands the thing which is good, that he may have to give to him that needeth.

²⁹ Let no corrupt communication proceed out of your mouth, but that which is good to the use of edifying, that it may minister grace unto the hearers.

³⁰ And grieve not the holy Spirit of God, whereby ye are sealed unto the day of redemption.

³¹ Let all bitterness, and wrath, and anger, and clamour, and evil speaking, be put away from you, with all malice:

³² And be ye kind one to another, tenderhearted, forgiving one another, even as God for Christ's sake hath forgiven you." (Ephesians 4; KJV)

I wanted to break this passage up, but it was perfect. It surely explains how we as individuals should grow and the manner in which we should fellowship based on the love, grace, and forgiveness we have received for CHRIST's sake. We are saved because CHRIST wanted it to be so. We are loved and forgiven because CHRIST wanted it to be so. He has seen us at our worst and saw the bride He will live with eternally. He loves us so much that He gave us his HOLY SPIRIT to indwell us, not to control us, but so we might know Him fully regarding his love for us. How many times have you thought to yourself, 'If I only I could just share my heart with the person I love, so they could know how much I love them'? You want them to know that you would give your life for them. Christ loves *us* so much that He did both. Not only did He die for us, but He put his Spirit in us, so we would know Him and not fear Him.

This is intimacy, as we turn away from foolish pursuits to understand the perfect order of GOD's creation. This ensures we can't be persuaded by the serpent in the garden. We will not build idols of pride. This ensures we will not forsake the promise and destroy the love that saves us. The book of Ephesians goes on to explain the relationship between CHRIST and the Church. The scripture uses the relationship between CHRIST and the Church to show the tender love and preparation essential for intimacy. I must share it:

> "*20 Giving thanks always for all things unto God and the Father in the name of our Lord Jesus Christ;*
> *21 Submitting yourselves one to another in the fear of God.*
> *22 Wives, submit yourselves unto your own husbands, as unto the Lord.*

23 *For the husband is the head of the wife, even as Christ is the head of the church: and he is the saviour of the body.*

24 *Therefore as the church is subject unto Christ, so let the wives be to their own husbands in every thing.*

25 *Husbands, love your wives, even as Christ also loved the church, and gave himself for it;*

26 *That he might sanctify and cleanse it with the washing of water by the word,*

27 *That he might present it to himself a glorious church, not having spot, or wrinkle, or any such thing; but that it should be holy and without blemish.*

28 *So ought men to love their wives as their own bodies. He that loveth his wife loveth himself.*

29 *For no man ever yet hated his own flesh; but nourisheth and cherisheth it, even as the Lord the church:*

30 *For we are members of his body, of his flesh, and of his bones.*

31 *For this cause shall a man leave his father and mother, and shall be joined unto his wife, and they two shall be one flesh.*

32 *This is a great mystery: but I speak concerning Christ and the church.*

33 *Nevertheless let every one of you in particular so love his wife even as himself; and the wife see that she reverence her husband"*

(Ephesians 5:20 – 33. KJV).

One of the most incorrectly used scriptures in the Bible is one where many have said, 'See, woman, it says right here: Wives submit yourselves to your husband,' not realizing if he has done all the preparation of laying down his life, washing her in love, and presenting her in her best light, he should not have to use the scripture. If he has done these things, she will know his heart and see GOD's authority.

Paul states in the scripture the relationship between CHRIST and the Church was a mystery. Paul did not have the rest of the story as it is given by John in Revelation. John goes on to speak about the Church as the bride of CHRIST. CHRIST is the groomsman who prepares the bride (which is the Church). There is intimacy with the Church as the Church completely surrenders to the order of GOD as Revelation says:

> "3 *And I heard a great voice out of heaven saying, Behold, the tabernacle of God is with men, and he will dwell with them, and they shall be his people, and God himself shall be with them, and be their God.*
>
> 4 *And God shall wipe away all tears from their eyes; and there shall be no more death, neither sorrow, nor crying, neither shall there be any more pain: for the former things are passed away.*
>
> 5 *And he that sat upon the throne said, Behold, I make all things new. And he said unto me, Write: for these words are true and faithful.*

6 *And he said unto me, It is done. I am Alpha and Omega, the beginning and the end. I will give unto him that is athirst of the fountain of the water of life freely.*

7 *He that overcometh shall inherit all things; and I will be his God, and he shall be my son."*

(Revelation 21:3 – 7, KJV)

We are cleansed in the blood of CHRIST and transformed through his death and resurrection, as we are baptized unto his death and resurrection. We are raised from the dead (after physical death) passing through the resurrection and faith of CHRIST. We are seen as overcomers—now the Sons of GOD, and we will be given of the fountain of the water of life. We shall live eternally, and we shall inherit all things.

The Bible is like a treasure hunt sometimes that speaks of the crowns, mansions, and treasures the faithful will receive in Heaven. All of our sorrows and pain shall be washed away. We can have great lives here on earth, as the faithful walking in GOD's order. We can receive a better life in Heaven, walking in His glory and basking in His light and His love.

If you have gotten this far in the book and do not know CHRIST as your personal Savior, now is the time to change that and get it right. Confess with your heart if you believe that JESUS CHRIST is the Son of GOD who walked the earth without succumbing to sin. He was killed, crucified on a cross, yet was raised from the dead, and He now sits at the right hand of POWER (GOD ALMIGHTY) praying for you and all of us that we might have life and have it more abundantly.

If you are saved and know the LORD died for you and cleansed you of sin, now is the time to listen to the HOLY SPIRIT and yield to it. Turn your life around and start living in the order God has created for you. It is time to stop malfunctioning and follow the code of your Creator. If you are abiding by the Word of GOD and living a fruit-filled life of blessing, it is time to share a life of significance by sharing your testimony with others, being light and salt extending yourself planting and watering more seed.

We live in a wicked time filled with divisive noise set on proving GOD is a lie and using differences to promote lies that render us judgmental and ineffective. Don't give in. It will not be comfortable speaking to hurting people who are malfunctioning in rebellion. We must remember we were once lost and, JESUS, in his grace and mercy, sojourns with us and feeds us, nourishing us. We are not fighting against flesh and blood (Ephesians 6:12), so put on the whole armor of GOD and restore folk with meekness and love. GOD is faithful. He is worthy of your faith, as He created you and He loves you. I pray peace and love on your walk and I will see you at the fountain in heaven. *Blessings.*

Chapter 12

Epilogue

W hen I started this book, it was because I was afraid of what America was becoming. I have neighbors talking to me about race wars and people preparing for civil war. I watch the fabric of America (its constitution) being discussed as if it may not have been perfect or its authors were not genuinely seeking equality through rule of law for *all* men. I have watched a great chasm created in men based on politics and economic viewpoints. There is candor that is threatening concerning global alliances and rumors of wars and conflicts. With all the conflict and erosion of social checks and balances, the question arises: What governs our interactions with each other? My son asked me, "why don't our molecules intertwine and we see folk who are half chair and half man? Why don't we phase into other rapidly moving molecules?" As we talk about everything on an atomic level, I understood there was an order in place throughout creation. If there is order, who gave the orders, or who established the order? There must be a divine architect. I understood the argument of the missing link, and learned behaviors of matter, as we see nothing in flux or evolving. I began to wonder how we can be so much alike and yet so fearful of each other.

I was in the Air Force (coolest name of any branch), and I got a new roommate who was white. He came into the room that I had been living in, but he did not speak. He was tentative in his movements and range of eye motion. I spoke and introduced myself. He said "hi," and he asked "if I listened to that music all the time." (It was Cameo's "Single Life" playing.) I responded, "That's my boom box. I can use earphones when you're in the room, but it plays what I like." He immediately left the room. Some thirty minutes later, he entered the room with the day Sergeant who was pissed. He yelled at me that I was not going to have a room by myself, and I had to accept that I was going to have a roommate. I told him I welcomed having someone to talk to, and explained what had happened.

He asked the young Airmen if my assessment was accurate, and he confirmed that my conveyance of the events was on point and accurate. The Sergeant (a white man) looked at the Airman and said, "You're wasting my time. You're going to have to learn to get along with folk that don't look like you. Buy your own boom box, get headphones, and listen to Hank Williams or whatever you want." He left and slammed the door as he left the room. The white Airman stood there looking at me awkwardly. I got up, left the room, and went and chilled with my buddy Sanders. Sanders was angry and went on to call them every kind of cracker he could think of. I decided I was going to get to know this guy and make him my friend.

When I got back to my room, there was another white guy in the room who explained that he had switched rooms with the first Airman. He was from California and didn't have a problem bunking with a brother. I introduced myself and began to chat with him about the whole thing. He explained the other white guy was from some small town in Georgia and was not used to being around Black folk in this capacity. He went on to say that the guy was trembling because he had been told we (Black men) had tails and would choke him to death in his sleep. I was like, "Get out of here." He had never seen *The Cosby Show*, *A Different World*, *Miami Vice* (Tubbs) or seen the movie *Sharky's Machine*. (I love Bernie Casey in that movie.) My mind was still made up. I was going to get to know that other guy, too. He wanted nothing to do with me.

I later started dating a beautiful blonde girl name Anne Miller from Highland Park, Detroit, and we got along on levels I didn't believe possible. She was fiercely loyal and protective and also had no reservations about making it clear that she was in love. We had taken a retreat to some cabins in the woods on an Air Force camping ground, and lo and behold the Airman was there with a bunch of friends. We all sat around and talked, smoked Marlboro Light cigarettes, played quarters, and drank beer. He loosened up after a while. He came over and sat by me and Anne and said to her, "I see why you chose him over all them other guys on base that wanted to date you. He's smart in class, he treats you well, and he is a good man. I can tell."

He said he had been watching me for weeks and determined that all his kin had taught him about Blacks was wrong. He didn't understand why this beautiful White lady had chosen to date me, a Black man, and why I had chosen her. He figured either of us could have anyone in our own race we wanted. He even admitted that he thought Anne was gorgeous. He had come to the conclusion that there's good White folk and good Black folk. Then there's bad White folk and bad Black folk.

We talked late into the night. Then Anne and I went to bed. She leaned over and kissed me and said, "What a freakin' Goober, that guy was. I can't believe you talk to him so long!" I wanted to—needed to—have him see me. Not to validate *me* but to see himself as wrong in his beliefs.

I had this relationship with many people of many races and backgrounds. I went on to hang out with a Latin brother, Sgt. Belasario, who drove a Supra and listened to Fog Hat and Airman Parker from Willacoochee, GA, who could play the dozen better than any Black man. And, there was Sgt. Banick and his cat (that was really a dog inside) named Butterball and Dan Whipple. From these relationships, I learned that we are all the same. I became friends with Asians, Indians, and Africans. At the end of the day we all are the same. The same in that we derive pleasure from favorable unions with each other, relish honesty and integrity, and are seeking to ensure our families live well. It is universal. It is universal because we are all human. There are cultures less trusting than others based on colonialism and media marginalization. There are stereotypes and unpleasantries bestowed upon most races as one race attempts to prove equality or superiority, which would stop if we all treated each other as equals and gave of ourselves so that others might live.

Then, later in my life, I witnessed President Obama become the first Black Man as President. (I put some respect on it.) I heard a pastor announce that, "Having a Black President meant the end of racism in America." I was not sure how he came to that conclusion but, as he went on to explain, I came to understand that he had no idea what racism was.

Racism was not over. It was in a stranglehold brought about by a new sense of "political correctness" that relegated racists to being "Goobers" (as Anne had said) or idiots as David Duke had been displayed as. In short, people had begun to eloquently express their racist view points, and we began to see something I had never seen before. Whites were confronting the establishment of advantage they had created and profited from and confessing that a diverse America was needed to be a better America.

While I saw racists vilify actions or behaviors stereotyped as Black and proliferate traditional "coonerism" entertainment and label it "urban" to further showcase the Black experience as alien and deficient. This display of stereotyped behavior was being embraced by other cultures and expressed in their way. It demonstrated to me that fear separated us, but there is something in us seeking to belong and to accept each other. I have Black friends who profess to be ultra conservatives, while ultra conservatives are seeking to separate themselves from Black folk as equals. They are girding up the platforms that have ensured white supremacy and white rule. (Black folk have a place. It is in subordination, it seems.). I watched White folk march with Black Lives Matter and rally in places where Black folk had been killed by white police.

Then, Trump was elected and racism was released from its stranglehold under the guise of "Making America Great, Again," and we saw xenophobia and racism emerge like a really pissed off imprisoned genie loosed from years of captivity. This is not GOD's plan for life! How did we get here?! Consolidated media outlets with a singular agenda? Corporate culture intent on ensuring its welfare and survival above social norms and negative externalities, translated into plain old greed? We are fearful and not living in GOD's order, and we are destroying our own homes with poor environmental choices, more concerned about the "now" than sustainable options. We don't know each other because we are listening to noise that filters our hearts' yearning to connect.

I met a lady recently with a Trump sticker on her car, and she told me of folk giving her the "finger," scratching her car, and being mean to her because of the bumper sticker. I asked her, why, then, keep it? She responded because she had a right to, regardless of whether she supported Trump any longer or not. Her property should not be damaged based on her sticker. I agreed with her. Yet, I further inquired if she was a true believer in Trump still. She did not answer fully, but did explain that she did not believe anyone had all the answers. I agree with her there, also, from a political standpoint, but CHRIST has all the answers, and He has given them to us. I tried to find the answers and give them to readers as I understand the issues and answers, which is all we can ask for anyone to do honestly.

After having navigated through interactions that have allowed me to have conversations, interactions, and relationships with people of all sorts of socio-economic diversities, I believe the truth and answers for harmonious coexistence is biblical. I do not believe we can coexist as we are, meaning having different gods, and religions, and agendas that we prop up above GOD's edicts and statutes expressed in the Holy Bible.

For example, I watched a Ted Talk recently were a lady was advocating pedophilia and was stating how she feels that it is natural. Well, anyone can feel anything. There has to be truth regulating social interactions. I also read an article on a prolific serial killer who kept speaking of his world (filled with poverty, drugs and despair and racial diversity) as opposed to answering the questions of the interviewing officer who was white and assumed that he was middle class and mainstream. His comments indicated that, as long as he murdered the weak and disenfranchised, he could continue because no one cared.

Unfortunately, the serial killer is right. We make it a point to wall up our hearts and our country from the ugly. We live in gated communities and gated private schools because we are fearful. And, rather than interact and find answers to help make change universal, we would rather relegate conditions to choices and imprison, wall off, and identify things that do not look like the 1% elite ruling class threats. This makes Blacks, Browns and other non-Whites are easier to profile, and it is easier to engage in the fear that separates us.

The universal answer is in the Bible, and what I hope I did was to share *who* GOD is and how his LOVE for us can save us and the world. If not to save your life, to save your eternal soul. My prayer is that your soul would dwell in Heaven. Heaven—a perfect peace after having lived a life of significance on earth. I am praying that you live by GOD's order, walking after the Spirit and not after the flesh. *Selah* (I always wanted to write something where I can close with that.)

REFERENCES

Albrecht, D. K. (October 2014). *Dr. Albrechts 5 Types of Fear: What We're Really Afraid Of...* Retrieved from The Coaching Tools Company.Com: thecoachingtoolscompany.com/5-types-of-fears-dr-karl-albrecht/

EEOC. (January 2018). *Facts about Discrimination in Federal Government Employment Based on Marital Status, Political Affiliation, Status as a Parent, Sexual Orientation, and Gender Identity.* Retrieved from U.S. Equal Employment: https://www.eeoc.gov/federal/otherprotections.cfm

Lynne Pepall, J. R. (August 2016). The "Veblen" effect, targeted advertising and consumer welfare. *Economics Letters Volume 145*, pp. 218 - 220.

ME, M. M. (September 2015,). *So How Many Times Is Fear Not Actually In The Bible?* Retrieved from Musing Of A Minister's Wife: musingofaministerwife.com/ministry/so-how-many-times-is-fear-not-actually-in-the-bible/

Paul, A. (n.d.). Hebrews chapter 126. *The Holy Bible.*

Paul, T. A. (n.d.). *The Book of Acts Chapter 2:41-47.*

Pope, M. H. (2008). Baal Worship. In *Encyclopedia Judaica*. Farmington Hills: The Gale Group & Centage.

Sledge, C. (2017). *Why You SHould Always Burn Your Ships*. Nashville: CharlesSledge.com.

Tarsas, P. o. (200). *Hebrews 4:12*. Rome.

Taylor, J. (1660). Doctor Dubitanitium or Rule of Conscience. In J. Taylor. London: Rivington 1868.